497
9091

BLOOMING INGENIOUS

BLOOMING INGENIOUS

BLOOMING INGENIOUS

The Impoverished Gardener's Guide

Angela Kirby

with drawings by Sandra Ireland
and diagrams by Serena Alexander

SOUVENIR PRESS

First published 1987 by Souvenir Press Ltd,
43 Great Russell Street, London WC1B 3PA
and simultaneously in Canada

ISBN 0 285 62796 1

Phototypeset by Rowland Phototypesetting Ltd,
Bury St Edmunds, Suffolk
Printed in Great Britain by
Redwood Burn Ltd,
Trowbridge, Wiltshire

CONTENTS

INTRODUCTION

Gardeners, you could say, are a mixed bunch. They come in shapes and sizes as many and varied as the plots they tend. Their tastes range from the classical through the rustic to the whimsical or even the bizarre; the apple of one gardener's eye is the next-door neighbour's eyesore. There is something, however, that nearly all of us have in common: less money than we need to carry out our plans—whether it means a few shillings for another packet of seeds, several pounds for the long-coveted shrub, or a couple of thousand here and there for antique urn or Gothick folly. Sooner or later we must learn to cut our costs, as well as the grass.

It would be ludicrous to suggest that a little ingenuity on the lines of 'why not knit yourself a garden gnome?' could solve all our problems, but there are many practical ways in which we *can* economise. These can be applied to even the most ambitious schemes, while, for simple plans, the possibilities are endless.

Some of these ideas will be obvious to us all. The more work that we are able to do ourselves, the more money will be saved. Help of any kind is hard to come by and skilled help is both rare and expensive. This is not to say that one should go for do-it-yourselfery at all costs, for some of those costs could become very high indeed. Be honest with yourself and, if the job is really beyond you, get in an expert to do it for you. In the long run, that will prove far less expensive than a botched-up bit of self-enterprise. Do not, however, give up too easily, as many a job, that at first sight might seem too difficult for the amateur, can be tackled if the necessary research and practice are carried out beforehand. Brickwork is a good example.

As for plants, the more we grow from seed and cuttings, and the more we beg, borrow and, I regret to say, steal, from friends, neighbours and the corporation park, the more we shall cherish them and, at the same time, feel a virtuous glow at our economy. True, not all of us will have the life-expectancy or the patience to grow a large tree from seed to maturity, but there *are* many plants that will romp away quite prettily in their first few seasons while we wait for their slower-growing relatives to oblige.

Not all of us could, or would, save up for a masterpiece of classical statuary dredged from the bed of the Aegean, but we *could* search through the end-of-year shows at the local art schools for a young sculptor whose work appealed to us, and either buy something from the show or commission a special piece.

Then again, we could go to evening classes and learn to make our own pots and urns whose imperfections might have more charm than the rigid symmetry of those polystyrene reproductions that are usually photographed, stuffed to overflowing with scarlet Salvias, grouped on patios made from polished marble off-cuts —another economy that I would not recommend to you. Savings should be made not by using cheap imitations, but by thorough research, careful planning and intelligent substitution when necessary.

During the last thirty or so years, I have had to cope with gardens ranging in size from rolling acres to about three square yards of damp basement area, complete with rotting window-boxes. I knew the effects that I wanted to achieve but had to come to terms with what was available in respect of time and money. There was never much of either to spare. I soon learned that it was essential to plan carefully if I was not to waste both.

The first point to decide upon is the *kind* of garden you want. That done, start your research; read all you can about the style you have chosen. There is no need to buy a large collection of books as these can be borrowed from friends and public libraries, but it *will* be worth your while to buy one good book on general garden practice. Some of the colour supplements and the gardening glossies are worth looking into for ideas, too. Flick through them on the bookstalls before buying, to see if there is anything in them on the sort of garden you have in mind.

You will be able to learn a lot from other gardens in your neighbourhood. You will see which plants flourish in the local conditions and which are sulking. Many useful ideas can be picked up from the gardens that you admire, and plenty of things to avoid from those which you do not. This research will be free, while, for a small outlay, it will be possible to visit some of the famous gardens round about. These can be a rich source of inspiration and most of them sell plants and seeds as well. Even when these gardens are very grand and your own very humble, there will still be plenty of ideas to copy. Unusual planting combinations of shape and colour, the use of local materials and small details of design and construction, can all be adapted for your own garden.

Having decided on the garden you want and with the initial research done, careful planning is essential, both on paper and by observation. Only when you are certain that your ideas will work in your own context should you start the basic construction. You may think that all this advance planning is much-ado-about-nothing, but I promise you that it is time well spent, the very foundation of blooming ingenuity and much more fun than it sounds (after all, most of it can be done indoors, with a glass in one hand). Should there be two or more of you involved in the project, it will have the additional advantage of establishing the areas of influence before you start. This should prevent much ill-feeling and overlapping, both of which can waste time and money.

One more bit of advice: learn to develop your 'eye' for the possibilities of other gardeners' rejects. Almost everything that you will need for making and embellishing your garden will be found, in time, on skips and tips. I have found earth by the yard, bricks by the ton, stone and concrete paving (both 'crazy' and regular), quarry-tiles, iron gates and railings, timber of all shapes, lengths and types, whole hedges and every kind of plant and container that you could imagine, as well as garden furniture. You will find turf from a garden that has been paved and paving from a garden that is being turfed—we are a wasteful nation—but more of this later. Above all, remember that your own enthusiasm, hard work and moments of sheer inspiration are free, all free.

1 DOWN TO EARTH

What kind of garden?

Choosing the type of garden that is right for you and for all those who will be using it regularly, is probably the most important decision that you will have to make. To begin with, it would be wise to consider all the styles that appeal to you and then to pick out one which could be made, with some chance of success, on the site and soil that you have, bearing in mind the amounts of time and money available to you. You will also have to choose a garden that will be compatible with your way of life and with the house it will surround. Erecting a rotunda at the end of the 30ft × 15ft plot of Number Two, Coronation Villas, will do nothing for either, while even the most engaging of gnomes will look more kickable than kitsch when sprawling over a Georgian terrace.

This, too, is the time to make an honest assessment of the time that you will have or will be prepared to spend on making and maintaining the garden. Remember that everything takes longer than you think and that there will be many other claims upon your time. The garden may well come way back in the queue and the odds are that you will end up with less time for it than you had estimated, rather than more. To make a garden that you are unable to keep up to the mark is a common and expensive mistake. Either the garden goes to seed or you have to pay someone else to look after it.

Be honest about your physical condition. Will your back stand up to hours of double digging, your knees to yards of hand weeding or your agility and balance to teetering about on a pair of high steps while you trim a ten-foot hedge or restrain a particularly rampageous rose? You may be fit and raring to go, but time creeps on as relentlessly as the bindweed. If you intend to stay in your garden for some years, look to the future and plan accordingly.

Then again, every regular user of the garden, whether two- or four-footed, will have to be taken into account. The elderly or handicapped, the young and the family pets will all have special needs which must be catered for to a greater or lesser extent if everyone is to get full value from the garden. Useless to weep for some demolished treasure, planted just where the three-year-old regularly ploughs his tricycle. A lot of grief and money will be saved by providing areas for everybody, with suitably robust planting where danger threatens. This, of course, will not prevent all accidents but it should reduce their frequency and severity. The following descriptions should give you some idea of the many types of garden that you could consider.

The formal garden

This is a very grown-up form of gardening and is not really a good idea if there are young children about, unless the place is big enough for them to have their own separate area and you have the perseverance to make them stay in it. At one end of the scale there will be stone fountains, balustrades, terraces, allées, parterres and more, much more. But in even the merest apology of a front garden, the same principles can be followed on an infinitely smaller scale.

In the first case, the economies made will be relative, for unless you have inherited the lot, in good nick, it will take all that you have, and probably more, just to stand still, let alone improve the place; you will need to be a very dedicated and fortunate 'searcher' to find classical columns and marble statues on the council tip, although it *has* happened. Nevertheless, there are savings to be made, even at this level. Terraces may be gravelled, rather than laid with stone; the urns could be terracotta or reconstituted stone (given one or two coats of liquid manure to tone them down), either of which would be cheaper than antique lead or hand-carved stone. Instead of statues, why not try topiary? A pyramid of Box

(*Buxus sempervirens*) or a peacock pruned from cheap and reliable old Privet (*Ligustrum vulgare*) could be handsome and charming. Even quicker and cheaper, Ivy can be trained up and over shapes made from chicken-wire, and clipped firmly into glossy perfection.

Small gardens and courtyards often benefit from the same sort of approach. Once established, it can be very labour-saving and not expensive to maintain. Take, for instance, the small front gardens found so often with terraced housing. These have to suffer the fumes of the passing traffic and the attentions of every passing animal, which will be convinced that they have been placed there for its convenience, in every sense of the word—a view that its wretched owner seems to share. Others will regard your garden as the ideal place to chuck their discarded fish-and-chip wrappings, empty Coke tins, meths bottles, cigarette butts and other more sinister offerings. Even if you have a pet-proof gate, nine out of ten visitors will forget to close it.

The front garden, therefore, is no place for the shy and the vulnerable; something much more robust is called for and a formal garden could be the right treatment. Almost the whole area could be paved with bricks, tiles, stone or a mixture of all three in a regular pattern. Gravel would be even cheaper and equally effective. Then plant a small evergreen hedge, kept close-clipped, which could be round, square or lozenge-shaped, surrounding a central feature which could be a pool, a statue or a mop-headed standard tree (Bay, Holly, Privet, Elæagnus, Euonymous), or maybe a weeper (Cherry, Pear, purple Willow, Rose, Cotoneaster). For more colour, pots planted up with bulbs and a succession of seasonable annuals could be placed round the garden in a regular pattern, while the central feature might be a larger tub, urn or chimney pot, planted out in the same manner.

If you have nothing more prepossessing to work on than a dank basement area or a small, dark, inner courtyard, give the walls a coat or two (the more the better) of paint, either white or some cheering colour—acid yellow, perhaps, or warm terracotta. Then, on the wall opposite the window which looks out on this area,

make a flat archway of trellis (made from battens you have salvaged from a skip, perhaps) and back it with a piece of old mirror.
Look in junk shops for the doors of shabby wardrobes, which will
give you the right size of glass. Use this archway to frame a
handsome Ali Baba pot, or a terracotta urn on a pedestal (which
you could make from wood or bricks), and make this a focal point
with one handsome plant—a Yucca or a Fatsia, perhaps. Alternatively, keep it stocked with a succession of bright plants and Ivy. As
it is the only vegetation you will have, you can afford to be
extravagant in the quality and number of plants, so that it is
positively bursting with life. The mirror will double the feeling of
light, colour and space in even the dreariest spot. Of course, if you
or any of your friends are handy with a brush, you could paint
some wonderfully colourful mural, perhaps in *trompe l'oeil*.

The cottage garden
This garden can be used in a surprisingly large number of situations. Seen at its best, perhaps, where it originated, in a glorious
riot of fruit, vegetables and flowers, surrounding a country
cottage, it can also be adapted very successfully to town gardening,
so long as all tendencies to the twee are firmly resisted: no mock
well-heads, wooden wheelbarrows planted with sizzling annuals,
and no miniature windmills.

Even the grandest house and garden can provide some corner
for a small cottage garden: outside the kitchen door, perhaps, with
Parsley edging the herb beds and pots of Basil and Nasturtiums on
the steps, where they will be to hand for salad making; in the
courtyard of the disused stables or surrounding the potting shed;
and, delightfully, within the green 'walls' of one of those outdoor
rooms so often seen in our famous gardens. The secret of successful cottage gardening is controlled chaos. Everything should seem
to romp away wherever the fancy takes it and no hint of the careful
maintenance should be seen. As most of the necessary materials
are either to hand or readily salvaged, and most of the plants
and vegetables can be grown from seed, it is a very economical

garden. Imagination and improvisation will come into their own.

The family garden
Probably the garden that most of us will have to accept at some time in our lives. Children, pets, flowers and vegetables will fight for life

within its boundaries. Often the result will be unsatisfactory, and an eyesore into the bargain, and this is where initial research and planning will pay real dividends. An honest approach is essential. It will be useless to place the play-area for small children at the far end of the garden, behind a Cupressus screen. No matter how expensive and enticing the equipment, they will not stay there but will be back, clinging to your ankles and clamouring for attention. If they are not, you will *know* that something awful has occurred, and will be forever darting off to the bottom of the garden in search of corpses. Sigh deeply, put the sandpit in the sunniest place you can find near to the house and they *will* spend happy hours in it. If you build it in neat brickwork it will not be too much of an eyesore and, when the children have grown out of it, you may turn it into a formal pool or a raised bed for alpines. Meanwhile, the sand will be less likely to sidle into the house when you are not looking.

Older children, on the other hand, will long to be as far away from you as possible, and will colonise every ramshackle shed, weeping tree or impenetrable thicket of bamboo, so try to leave a 'wild' corner for them somewhere.

The vegetable garden can be placed farther away, behind a hedge or screened by espalier-trained fruit trees, but both the dustbins and the compost heap should be sited where you can stomp out to them in even the dirtiest of weather. As for the clothes-line, wherever you put the damned thing it will prove an irresistible attraction to the partially-sighted, bicycling children, cat-chasing dogs, wheelbarrowers and your neighbour's bonfire smoke, but you can at least *try* to find a safe spot for it with-in sprinting distance of the kitchen door, for when the clouds inevitably burst.

I know to my cost that it is not a good idea to have the greenhouse next to the lawn where the children will play cricket and croquet, while the swimming-pool and the tennis court, if you run to such things, should be as far away from the house as possible; in this climate they are a depressing sight for most of the year and are better forgotten when not in use. If you insist on squeezing a swimming-pool into a small garden, do resist the temptation to have a bright blue liner. This may look dashing enough under a blazing sun but it can be very unnerving, like an unwinking eye, in the softer light of an English summer.

I am also of the opinion that barbecuing is a very overrated pastime; for my purposes, a small, Hibachi-type portable barbecue which can be kept in the garden shed when not in use, is a far better bet than one built like a brick stove just outside the French windows. If you must have one, try to site it where it will not blow grease-laden smoke all over the Laura Ashley mix'n'match and where, in the winter, you will not see it, squatting gloomily like a build-your-own mausoleum.

The low-maintenance garden

An ideal garden for the elderly, lazy or those who work long hours and need the place for relaxation and perhaps entertaining. Once established, it should require very little time and effort to keep it looking at its best. I hate to nag about this but, once again, it is the initial planning which will make all possible.

The traditional lawn is out, since even the smallest lawn takes more time and effort than any other part of the garden except, perhaps the rockery—but who would want one of those? If you must have something that looks like a lawn, in sunny places try Camomile 'Treneague', some of the creeping Thymes or *Raoulia tenuicaulis*, planting them in light soil to which you have added some coarse sand or grit. You will have to weed between them until they have dug their toes in and begun to spread themselves about a bit, but after that it will be a brave weed that breaks their ranks. In a shady place, clipped Ivy or the tiny Helxine (Mind-your-own-business) are the answer, although the latter will not endure too much wear and tear. In a small courtyard or roof garden, you can go all out for artifice and have one of the imitation grasses. Be careful about the colour—some of them are rather too bright—but there is a very nice shade of silvery-olive which is most dignified and restrained. It does not mind sun or shade, can be hosed or hoovered and is exceptionally popular with sunbathers.

If you absolutely insist on grass, set narrow strips of it between rows of brickwork or paving. These can be mown or clipped quite quickly and there will be little or no edge clipping to be done.

Some form of paving is another solution, whether in a single material or, if the area is largish, in a mixture of several—stone, brick, cobbles and gravel—with plants growing up through the surface here and there. A pool or water garden, once made and planted, will need little attention. Well stocked with plants, water snails and fish, it will give a great deal of pleasure and will look after itself most of the time, if you keep it clear of fallen leaves.

All plants will need some care and attention in their first year or two, but some are more resilient than others. In any case, it is important to have an outside tap, at the very least, to make watering easier, if you cannot run to a fully automatic watering system.

In a small garden, it may be that you will only need one good specimen tree or large shrub. Choose one of the so-called 'architectural' plants: those which are handsome in form and foliage. They are most often evergreen and keep their good looks throughout the year. This is important if the garden is used in winter or is in constant view. Camellias, Fatsias, Mahonias and Yuccas are all good examples of this type of plant. Then, with one or two containers planted out with a succession of bulbs and annuals, placed near the house where they can be watered easily, you will have a garden of maximum impact achieved with the minimum of effort. Even the most ham-fisted can make and maintain this type of garden in a most economical fashion.

The ultimate in low maintenance is the painted garden. This is perfect for the young and itinerant. Walls or a portable back-drop are painted with murals—classical, tropical, surreal or of nursery-rhyme simplicity. Plants and ornaments are painted on to wooden cut-outs (marine ply would be best) and placed cunningly between large containers of real plants. Trellis and mirror can add to the

PAVING PATTERNS

Stones or slabs, plants, cobbles, bricks,
setts or tiles, and gravel.

illusion, imitation grass is a must (here you *could* use the bright green one) and the whole lot can be packed up and moved on to the next dreary squat or dingy basement flat, re-erected, given a new lick of paint here and there, perhaps, and be back in business the same day. Made with old off-cuts of wood from skips, etc., and using any number of left-over bits of paint, it can be a long-lasting and incredibly cheap way to brighten up your life and living quarters.

Gardening for the elderly or handicapped

These ideas can be applied to the whole garden or, if others also use it, to just a part. Various physical problems will demand special solutions, but some general principles will apply to most situations. All surfaces should firm, even and non-slip, with shallow steps or gentle slopes and ramps if wheelchairs are in use. Plants and vegetables can be grown in raised beds made from bricks, breeze-blocks, railway sleepers or peat-blocks. The garden pool can be raised in a similar fashion, but make sure there is enough room between them for a wheelchair to pass through. If the garden is to be used by the blind or partially sighted, make sure that the paths and terraces are kept clear of low branches and of plants with prickles, spines and thorns. Plant as many sweet-smelling trees, shrubs and plants as possible and try to include the sound of running water and perhaps a piece of sculpture that would stand up to being handled. For those in wheelchairs, plants that attract butterflies would be a bonus and so would a bird-bath and bird-table. The birds and butterflies would appreciate them, too.

The time to plan and begin to make this kind of garden is in middle age. This may sound a little morbid, but age comes to us all, together with some degree of diminished energy and vigour, if not actual disablement. Plan the garden for the future and start the work while you still have the strength and enthusiasm to carry out the changes. Not all at once, of course, but bit by bit as each area comes up for renovation. Carefully done, the whole thing should

look as if you had chosen that style for aesthetic reasons alone. Its real purpose will remain your secret for years to come.

The wild garden

You may think that you have got one of these without trying; certainly you should think twice before removing any existing plants when going for this type of garden. Mark them all on your plan (see Chapter 2) with a pencil and then try rubbing out some of them to achieve some natural-looking glades and groupings. Old fruit trees and even the common Lilac and Privet can have attractively gnarled trunks which have developed interesting shapes. Keep some of these to add character to the garden; a little thinning can help to display them to advantage. Paths should wind round groups of trees and shrubs to give the illusion of further depth. As always, include some evergreen trees and shrubs to add the deep notes to the picture and let all sorts of plants, both wild and cultivated, sprawl blowsily between them. Climbers should crawl lovingly over undistinguished or dead trees; bulbs can pop up through and die down gracefully in patches of rough-mown grass; paths can be of grass, gravel, sawn logs, crushed bark or stones; fences should be informal and partially hidden by the rampaging greenery. The whole thing should look as if, like Topsy, it 'just growed', but you will probably spend happy hours restraining its enthusiastic advances and planning new surprises round each corner: a silent, secretive pool, a stream of Bluebells, a hidden seat or gazebo . . . what could be simpler or more delightful? Most of the trees and plants will be native to these islands, and so will grow happily and without fuss. They will be cheap to buy and many can be grown from seed.

There are other gardens, of course, and you will undoubtedly come upon them in your researches, but those described above should give you some idea of what can be done on a limited budget, without too much difficulty or back-breaking labour.

2 CUNNING PLOTS

Planning

The more care and time that you devote to this stage, the more smoothly your garden will take shape, and the fewer expensive errors there will be. Mistakes will be made, of course; we all make them, whether through ignorance, carelessness or the sheer perversity of life in general, but we can reduce them to a minimum and, with any luck, avoid the more ruinous ones.

Having done all the preliminary research and decided upon the type of garden you want, your next step is to make a plan. Get hold of some squared paper, either graph-paper or the kind that dressmakers use to cut patterns from. Both types can be bought from most large stationers, but if you cannot find them you can make something similar. Use lining paper, or old wallpaper (plain side up, of course) and cut it to fit a pin-board, either one that is purpose-made, usually from felt-covered cork, or one that you have made yourself by glueing cork tiles to off-cuts of wood or hardboard. I find that about 60cm ×75cm (24″ × 30″) is a convenient size. Use drawing-pins to fix the paper firmly to the board and then draw a grid on the paper. The size of the squares will depend on the size of your garden, but the bigger the scale the better. 1/50 is usual for small gardens, 1/100 for larger ones. Each square on the grid will represent a unit of measurement, either metric or Imperial. Older properties will have been constructed on the Imperial scale, so you may find it easier to work in that. More modern properties will probably be metric, so work accordingly. Whichever type of measurement you use, most builder's merchants and other tradesmen will be able to work out the necessary conversions when you order materials, if you find this beyond you.

Measure out your plot carefully. If your garden is regular in shape, this will be an easy job, but if it is large and irregularly-shaped, things will be a little more complicated, so check first to see if there are any existing plans. Sometimes they are attached to the deeds, and if an architect has been used at any time for the building or alterations, he or she may well have drawn in the outlines of the plot. If not, you will have to resort to a system of measurements called triangulations. For this you will need a good, long measuring-tape, some skewers to hold it in place, a builder's square (a larger version of a set-square, which you can make yourself), a spirit-level and a home-made measuring-pole to mark changes of level, some line (string or clothes line will do) and canes or skewers to hold it. With these, you can do the job single-handed, although it will be quicker and easier with two people.

To fix the boundaries and the position of the house and other features within them, start by measuring outwards from a face or angle of the house to a boundary line, then measure some distance along the boundary and, from there, back to the house at the spot from which you started.

Continue round the house like this until you have built up an accurately measured plan. If the garden is a large one, you can work from the house to any fixed point such as an outbuilding, tree or wall, in the same fashion. On any empty site, where no such fixed points exist, make your own by driving a stake into the ground, or make two parallel lines of stakes and, by measuring between them and out from them to the boundaries in a series of triangles, an accurate set of measurements can be drawn up and transferred to your plan, noting down any significant internal measurements as you go. You will need to mark in the boundaries, the house and outbuildings (including doors and windows), plus any features that you intend to retain: water, large trees, walls, hedges, entrances and exits, terraces and paths, etc.

If the site is level you will be able to take the measurements with a tautly-held tape at ground level, but if the levels vary you will have

TRIANGULATION

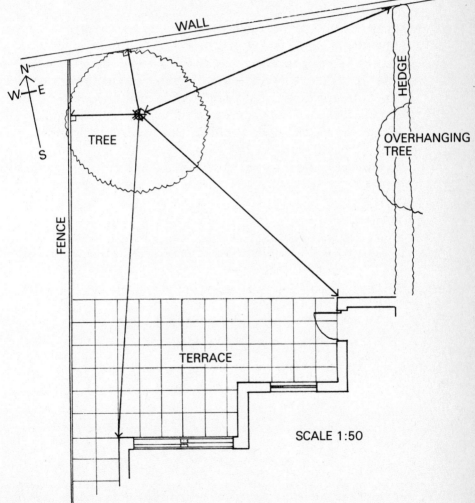

WALL

N
W—E
S

HEDGE

OVERHANGING
TREE

TREE

FENCE

TERRACE

SCALE 1:50

to take the measurements at a higher point, checking the line with a straight-edge and a spirit-level as you go. This method can also be used to plot the fall of the land, and a sectional drawing of this should be made and marked in on the margins of your plan, as this will be a help when it comes to planning and estimating for steps and retaining walls, etc.

Remember to leave enough room around your plan to mark in any features on neighbouring land that will affect yours—an eyesore to be screened out, a beautiful view to be opened up, a handsome building to be 'framed', or trees that overhang and cast shade on your land. When drawing in existing trees, note both the position of the trunks and the dimensions of the spread of the branches or 'canopy', as this will affect your planning and planting. (See diagram, p. 25.)

If you do not know where your drains and main service supply lines are, make sure that you find out, either from your builder or

MEASURING GRADIENTS

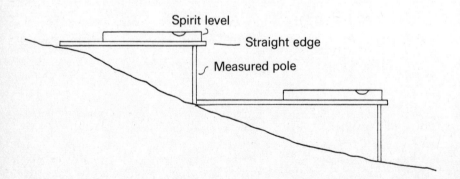

from the relevant authorities, before carrying out any major works. Mark their positions on your plan with dotted red lines and remember to check back to them as the work goes on. Man-holes should also be drawn in; they must be accessible and are expensive to move, but can often be disguised by plants or containers, and can sometimes be raised or lowered a little to fit in with the changed levels (see p. 75). Make notes in the margins of areas of light and shade in the garden at various times of the day, for example, morning sun, shade at mid-day etc., throughout the year, as well as notes of the prevailing winds, frost pockets and, of course, north, south, east and west. It is also a good idea to note down any peculiarities of the soil, such as boggy ground, dry shade, and acid or alkaline soil. In larger gardens, there may be several variations like this in different parts of the plot.

With the site plan finished and the necessary notes made, you are ready for the next stage. Place a piece of tracing paper over your plan on which you will plot the changes and improvements to be carried out. Work in pencil to begin with, as there are sure to be some false starts and alterations to make as you go along. However, before you draw anything on the tracing paper, walk round the garden with a pencil and paper, making sketches and notes, trying various new ideas and roughing out how you think they will look from different points of view. It is a good idea to look out onto the garden from an upstairs window, as this will give you another and useful perspective. If your garden has a view or can be provided with one by some judicious thinning and pruning, your plan will to some extent be predetermined, as your main sight-lines will lead towards this prospect. In other gardens, the focal point will be within: a fine tree or shrub, an ornament or perhaps a pool. If there is no such point of interest, you will have to provide one and plan around it, either formally or informally, as your fancy runs.

It is a good idea to take some photographs of the house and garden from different angles and have several prints made of each aspect. On these, you can draw, in ball-point, various improvements and changes: a pair of planted urns on the front steps, a garden seat across a corner, a large tree underplanted with shrubs, a trellis or a climber on a wall. If all this strikes you as an extravagant gesture, just remember how much an expensive mistake will cost—an unnecessary load of topsoil, a terrace or path mis-sited, a pool in deep shade—these could all lead to an excessive use of cash-points in an attempt to stay clear of your bank manager's cold blue eyes.

Incidentally, when sketching out your ideas, set your view at an angle, rather than head on. It is easier to do this way, and can give a more realistic effect. If you think of a shoe box, set askew, with the long side nearest you, missing, you will get the idea.

In a larger garden, you can plan for a number of these 'stage-sets' and route your paths so that you come across them unexpectedly: a pavilion or a shaded seat in one corner, a rose or herb garden in another, a wild garden in a third, and so on. In our climate, it is a good idea to provide seating in areas of both light and shade. If you are at home during the day, place the sunny seating area where the sun falls at noon, but if you are at home in the evenings only, site the seating area accordingly. However, even our most predictable summers can provide some days of searing heat, so if you have room to put a bench in the shade somewhere, it will provide cool relief.

This is the time to decide on where you are going to place the 'utility' areas (a horrible expression, but I cannot think of another one)—the greenhouse, garden shed, compost heap, clothes-line, dustbins, sandpit, barbecue, *et al*—if your garden is large enough for such things. A greenhouse, or at least a cold frame, will be an invaluable aid in propagating plants, whether by seed or by cuttings, and will certainly help to keep to a minimum the cost of planting out your garden. On the other hand, today's models are seldom things of beauty, and the problem is to hide the brutes without starving them of the light they need. In a large garden, this is not too difficult; they can be banished to an unfrequented corner and hidden by a hedge or something, but in a small space it is a

HOW TO DRAW A 3D PLAN

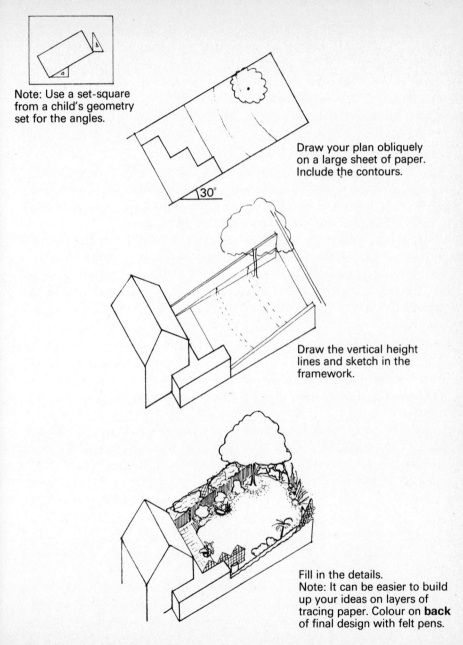

Note: Use a set-square from a child's geometry set for the angles.

Draw your plan obliquely on a large sheet of paper. Include the contours.

30°

Draw the vertical height lines and sketch in the framework.

Fill in the details.
Note: It can be easier to build up your ideas on layers of tracing paper. Colour on **back** of final design with felt pens.

different matter. They will sit there malevolently, staring at you in a disconcerting way, and I for one would prefer to do without them, remembering that small miracles of fertility can be achieved by sowing seed into everything from an egg-box to a hollowed-out grapefruit, and 'bringing them on' in airing cupboards, glassed-in porches and warm window-sills.

Garden sheds are a different matter as they do not have the same need for light, so that a cunning bit of planting will obliterate them. Evergreens can be grown up their sides, and climbers can sprawl amorously across their roofs, but do remember to give them, and all of these areas, a good firm base and a well-constructed path which will make access safe and easy in bad weather.

If you have room for a kitchen garden, so much the better. Once again, a good path is essential, and the beds should be divided by more paths to make it easy to work on and harvest from them. A good open site with plenty of light is necessary, and while I would not suggest that you place it right in front of the drawing-room windows, a well designed and planted-out kitchen garden can be most charming, if it is kept in good heart. Nevertheless, no matter how well managed and rotated, there will be many times when there is more bare earth than greenery to look at, so remember this when thinking romantically of those photographs of old potagers. However, the beds may be edged with herbs: the Sages, perhaps, or alternate plants of green and gold Thyme, with Parsley, Chives or with Alpine Strawberries. I am not sure that home-grown vegetables are much of an economy, if one costs one's time realistically, and allows for losses from disease, predators and waste, but they are undoubtedly fresher, more delicious, and probably better for you, as you can at least be sure that they are free from sprays or chemicals; and, of course, you can eat them not merely with butter, but with a fine seasoning of virtue and self-congratulation.

If you have no room for a separate vegetable patch, quite a few things can be grown in mixed borders, pots, window-boxes and other containers. The smallest spot can house a few herbs, and

Runner Beans will climb up walls and trellises as happily as they will up bean poles. Clumps of Rhubarb, Horseradish, Angelica and Globe Artichoke will provide handsome foliage in any odd corner, while Strawberries will flourish in a special pot or barrel if they are well looked after.

A fruit tree can be trained against a wall, whilst one that is grown on dwarf stock will fit charmingly into any but the merest pocket hankerchief of a plot, as will one of the crab-apple trees with edible fruit, such as 'John Downie' or 'Golden Hornet'. These have the added bonuses of blossom in the spring and brightly coloured fruits in the autumn, through into winter, which will provide you with the most delicious jelly. Fruit trees can also be trained flat, along wires, to make a fence, to edge a path or screen a vegetable

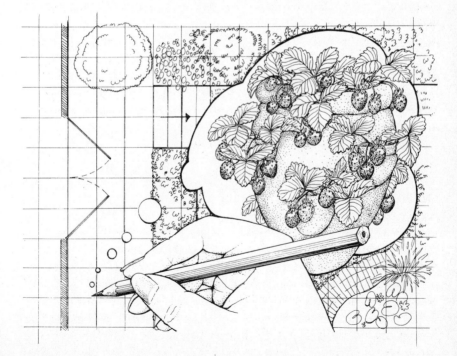

bed, but if you live in rabbit country, you will have to make more serious efforts to seal off the vegetable garden.

Try to make room for a compost heap. You can make your own bins from bricks, breeze-blocks, timber or just chicken-wire nailed to posts. If you really cannot find room for even a small bin, you can fill plastic refuse sacks with garden and kitchen waste, tie them firmly at the neck and dump them in some hidden corner to rot down—behind the shed, perhaps, or hidden by a clump of ever-greens.

In even the smallest of gardens, you will have to find somewhere for the dustbins to stand, and if possible, make some kind of 'hide' for them. They should not be too far from the kitchen door, with a good path to them, and any disguise that you plan for them will have to be sufficiently robust to withstand the onslaught of the dustmen, who regard this sort of frippery as a challenge to their masculinity.

A home must be found for garden tools and deck chairs, etc. If the garden is too small for a shed and you have no garage, a spot in the house will have to be selected. A broom cupboard, cellar or that handy space under the stairs are all possibilities. In older prop-erties, there is often an outside privy, and this makes a splendid toolshed. If the 'seat' is still intact, it will prove an ideal place for a little peace and quiet when all else fails:

> Far from the storms that shake the great,
> Contentments shall fan my seat . . .
> (Cowper)

When you are quite sure that you have found a practical spot for all of the above that you can accommodate, mark them on your plan (still in pencil).

This will be a good time to mark in those things that you wish to remove, so draw them in with dotted blue lines, but do not rush these decisions or take drastic action before you are quite sure what you want to knock down or uproot. An overgrown shrubbery, for instance, could, if carefully pruned, provide you with some small trees or large shrubs that have developed handsomely twisted trunks and branches, and these could be just the pivot on which to hang your design. Once cut down, their possibilities will be lost forever. A fruit tree that is a little long in the tooth could still make a splendid support for a clambering rose or clematis as, indeed, could an old tree stump, and it will be a great deal less expensive to put them to work in this way than to go to the trouble of having them removed. A tree or shrub that is in 'just the wrong place' might, if the overall planting plan were changed, prove to be in just the right place.

Even an ugly wall or outbuilding can be painted or trellised, perhaps, and smothered in climbers. In fact, most structures which will provide a surface for vertical climbers can be turned into an asset, and many plants will be grateful for the added protection. You might think that nothing could redeem the ugliness of chain-link fencing or wire, fixed to concrete posts, but when their depressing nakedness is veiled by ivy or an evergreen honey-suckle, they are transformed into handsome green walls.

It is even more important to go carefully before levelling the ground. Are you quite sure that you want it level? Of course you will want to fill in pot-holes, etc., but a change of levels can be an attractive feature in a garden, even if it is just a few inches to provide a couple of steps from one area to another. A tree or a gentle mound will give instant height to your plan, and possibly help to hide an ugly building, whilst even an inconvenient tilt or slope can be terraced by the cut-and-fill method (see p. 66). In a small town garden, a series of small terraced beds can provide far more shape and interest than a flat design. However, whether you do decide to level or to change levels, remember that you will have to remove the topsoil first and set it aside for re-use later on. Topsoil is precious and should be preserved whenever possible. In general, you will find a use for most excavated material, and this is all to the good: the less stuff you have to barrow away to a skip, or take in your protesting car to the council tip, the better for you.

Talking of skips, should you decide you need one (and they are not cheap), you will have to obtain a skip permit from the engineering department of your local council, in order to have it placed in the road. (If you have parking meters in the road, you will also have to pay for the privilege of parking your skip: the 'temporary lifting of parking restrictions', as they put it.) You will have to provide it with warning lights at both ends during lighting-up hours, and I would recommend that you pay a little extra to have a tarpaulin put over it at night. If you do not, you may wake up to find that your brand-new skip has been, like the widow's cruse, miraculously refilled. People with rubbish to dispose of develop the nose and cunning of lecherous curs. They will scent out your skip from miles away, arrive in the dead of night, hurl in their debris, then screech away on burning rubber before you can point out to them, courteously, that you have paid good money for the skip and would like to be able to use it yourself.

It is true that you may find something useful amongst their cast-offs, but more often than not they will have left you a collection of plastic bags from Sainsbury's and Waitrose, stuffed to overflowing with empty gin bottles, lethal sardine-tins and dubious-looking tights.

When planning out the areas around the house, it is important to realise that all surfaces that abut the house should be at least six inches below the damp-proof course. If you don't know where it is, get a builder to check for you. As a rough guide, it is usually a few inches below the door-sills. It is essential not to 'bridge' the d.p.c. in any way—by allowing the earth from wall-beds to mound up over it, for instance, or by laying paving above it. If you wish to make a raised bed along a house wall, or a new wall butting onto the house, you will need to install a vertical d.p.c. to avoid the risk of penetrating damp, and if you are not a skilled and knowledgeable do-it-yourselfer, get professional advice or you could run into some very expensive problems.

All paths and terraces should have a slight fall or camber to prevent surface waters lying on them. This fall should be away from the footings of the house and into the drainage system through drain-traps, or into soak-aways.

On areas away from the house, the water can drain into surrounding lawns or planting areas, unless the water-table is already too high, in which case you will have to consider installing some form of drainage system: a soak-away or a French drain if the problem is patchy, or a serious system of land-drains if the problem is an overall one. If the wetness is caused by over-compacted soil and subsoil, it may be possible to deal with it by digging over the land, breaking up the subsoil and incorporating as much vegetable matter in the bottom spit of each trench as you can lay your hands on, together with as much coarse grit and gravel as you can afford; do not, however, be tempted to do this just round the roots of a tree or shrub that you are planting, as this will form a sump into which water will drain, and your plant will become waterlogged and drown. Suitable materials to add to the broken-up subsoil include broken bricks, shards and stones, twiggy trimmings, seaweed, bracken, cabbage stalks, corn husks, straw, bark and compost. Into the topsoil you can fork peat, compost, coarse grit, leaf mould and well rotted manure. If the vegetable matter that you use is not sufficiently decomposed, it could produce a nitrogen deficiency in the soil and you will have to correct this with a suitable fertiliser.

For larger areas with a more serious problem, a herring-bone system of land-drains should be laid at a minimum of 45cm (18″) deep, bedded-on, and surrounded by gravel which will allow the water to seep through into the open-jointed pipes. These should slope in a continuous fall to soak-aways at the lowest points of the garden. Where the garden is small and the damp less severe, a few soak-aways or French drains in the worst parts should do the trick. A soak-away is a hole roughly 90cm–120cm (3ft–4ft) square and deep. Fill the bottom with large stones and hardcore, to about half of its depth. Then add a layer of gravel and top this with a layer of upturned turfs; finally, replace the topsoil and the turf. A French drain is similar in principle, being a ditch which is filled with stones and gravel, leading the water away from the boggy patch.

In a large garden, you could consider planting some kind of thirsty tree, such as a Willow, Poplar, Oak or Cherry. These will suck up surplus moisture and, by transpiration, release it into the atmosphere. However, these trees have invasive roots, which can undermine drains and foundations; even, in periods of drought, causing the subsoil to shrink, which can lead to the subsidence of the buildings, a very expensive disaster to remedy. The root system of a tree can spread well beyond its canopy, so that, as a rough guide: do not plant poplars within 150 feet of any drains or buildings; with an oak, 100 feet is probably safe. In a small, damp garden, you might think it worth while to build some raised beds, about one or two feet high, in which the plants could grow safely with no fear of waterlogging. These have the added advantages of changing the levels in the garden and are very easy to maintain, which makes them especially suitable for the elderly, handicapped or even just those with back problems (and there are many of us around).

There is a new system of land drainage which I have not yet used but which has had favourable mentions in the gardening press. This has a crush-proof core of flexible styrene, wrapped in a rot-proof filter which is laid in a comparatively tiny trench, 10cm (4") wide by 25cm (10") deep. This obviously causes far less disturbance of the garden, can be done easily enough by an amateur and is claimed to be cheaper than the conventional clay pipe drains.

As well as the drainage system, you will have to make some provision for watering. For anything more demanding than a couple of containers, I would beg you to splurge out on an outside tap at least. If you have a plumber around doing odd jobs, it is not very expensive to get him to install one for you. If you have a largish garden, and your house is more or less in the middle, try to have an outside tap on all sides. The initial expense will be repaid by the savings on plants. Even in our sodden climate, there are surprisingly long periods of dry and windy weather when daily watering is necessary. I find, time and time again, that unless people are fanatical gardeners, watering is hardly ever carried out sufficiently or frequently enough, unless it is made very easy to do. When they get back from work, the kitchen sink and taps are needed for the preparation of the evening meal and washing up or rinsing through the smalls, so that it is not convenient to have it cluttered up with watering-cans and hose-pipes which, no matter what smart gadget you use to fix them to the tap, almost inevitably work loose at some stage, to the great detriment of the kitchen and its occupants. Consequently, the watering gets put off . . . and off . . . and off. Given an outside tap and, whenever possible, a wall-mounted hose reel and some kind of sprinkling device, the laziest of us will be prepared to turn on the tap and, from time to time, move the sprinkler round the garden. The salvation of a newly planted hedge, turfed lawn, or ten containerfuls of bedding, will soon recoup the cost of the whole installation.

In very large gardens you will have to join up a series of hose-pipe lengths, using those cunning little connectors (that seem designed to frustrate and foil me), but you will have to take care that the resulting serpent does not strangle your most precious plants in its undulating coils or knock down your containers like nine-pins as it writhes across your patio. Incidentally, you can often pick up hose-pipes, and all sorts of garden equipment, quite cheaply at auctions held in private houses, from the humblest to the grandest pile. In the latter case, the dealers have come for the *objets d'art*, leaving the more humdrum household and garden effects to be sold off in job lots, and this is where the bargains are to be found, especially if the weather is foul enough to frighten off any but the determined buyer. If you are installing some kind of fixed irrigation system, or stand-pipes in various parts of the garden, you will have to protect them from frost by burying the pipes about 90cm (3ft) down and lagging the stand-pipes, unless the system can be drained down in the winter.

An electricity supply is something else that you may find it useful to install, but this is really something for an electrician to do, requiring special cable and fittings. At first, you may think this a bit of a luxury in terms of economical gardening, but this is not really the case. If you have to move round your garden at night, for any reason, searching for a lost pet or a recalcitrant child (or spouse), perhaps, or to-ing and fro-ing to garage and log pile, well-lit paths and terraces, especially when a change of levels is involved, will be a big safety factor, while efficiently lit exits and entrances are good burglar deterrents, which could be your most cost-effective ploy of all. Other possible needs are lighting and power points to garages, greenhouses and sheds.

An electrically-heated propagator could make for real savings in stocking the garden. If you plan to have a pool with a fountain, or water splashing from a wall-mask into a shallow pool or basin (both of which you could make yourself), you will need electricity to power the submersible pump. Lights on the terrace will turn it into a magic dining-room at night, while various points of interest round the garden, such as a pool, tree or spectacular plant, will all take on new and mysterious life when suffused by strategically placed up-lighters or 'spots'. The burbling and splashing of moving water will be an endless delight and fascination and, at the very least, all these 'luxury' additions will enhance the enjoyment of the garden and the value of your property. They are seldom as expensive as improvements inside the house.

All these services—drains, water and electricity—will be most easily and therefore most cheaply, installed at the earliest possible moment in the garden's construction or re-construction, especially if the necessary tradesmen are about the place already, working in the house. You need not add all the equipment straight away. The fountain, lights and propagator, etc., can all be bought and added at a later stage, but you will have got the services in and out of the way, with all the necessary disturbances over, so that there will be no need to upset the, by then, we hope, established garden and plant-life. As for the drains, if there is a need for them, you will realise, if you have ever seen a gardenful of dying, water-logged plants, that they are not a luxury but a necessity.

Once all these have been decided upon, pencil them in on the tracing paper, and start to mark in your other ideas: walls to be built, paths and terraces, trees, planting areas, lawns, ponds, even the garden furniture and ornamental items.

This basic plan will help you to see if your ideas make sense in a practical way . . . that the paths, for instance, are wide enough and that they are taking a realistic route which has some likelihood of being followed; that the terrace will provide enough room for sunbathing and dining out, or for the children to rollerskate to self-destruction; have you hung the clothes-line in an area of permanent shade? etc., etc.

When you have sorted all these problems out on paper, and have added all the features that you can cram in, try to visualise your creation three-dimensionally. Imagine a tree standing sentinel here, a path disappearing round a corner there, somewhere, perhaps, a gleam of water; referring back to your photographs and preliminary sketches.

If this vision is beyond you, set out your plan with pieces from a child's toy garden or with the accessories for model railways. If you do not have either of these, and are unable to borrow them, draw all the features and plants on the plan (or cut out pictures from magazines and catalogues) keeping roughly to scale and mount them on cardboard. Move these around like a stage set. Then kneel down by the table and look through this set at eye-level, which should give you some idea of how the finished garden will look when it is established. If it looks overcrowded you will be able to remove a tree here, an ornament there, shift things round a bit until you feel that you have the balance of the place just about right. This all sounds like a great deal of toil and trouble; in practice it is a lot less bothersome than you would think. In fact, it is all rather good fun, and a great deal more entertaining than most TV programmes, while, once again, it will help to weed out potentially expensive mistakes and a lot of wasted time and effort.

Armed with your plans, sketches and photographs, and with your stage set firmly in mind, you can begin to try it all out 'on the ground'. Use lengths of string or hosepipes to lay out paths, lawns and flowerbeds. Use bricks, stones and pebbles to mark out clumps of planting within these lines. Stick large twiggy branches into the ground to represent trees and shrubs and lay out black refuse sacks or plastic sheeting to suggest water. This may sound rather child-ish, but it is amazing how the garden will take shape for you. Pieces of household furniture can stand in for their outdoor cousins and so can indoor plants and containers. Lengths of material strung over string can suggest the lines of a hedge or fence, while cardboard grocery boxes or tea chests can indicate raised levels and

low walls. Not only will this be a real help to you but it will also provide your neighbours with hours of innocent pleasure and entrance any children or animals who may chance upon you.

Ideally, all the preliminary research and planning should be done in times of rotten weather, when it is too cold and wet to work outside. However, life seldom works out so neatly and you may well have to get the whole job done in a mad rush during the year's one heatwave, when your only desire is to be sipping Pimm's on the postulated patio. Fortunately, in these days of container-grown plants, a garden can be made at any time when the ground is not actually frozen, waterlogged, or drought-stricken.

However, at whatever season you begin, do not attempt to implement your plans until you have checked that you will not be infringing the law, or local by-laws. All new buildings, including outbuildings, greenhouses, walls and even large sheds may need planning or building permission—probably both—so check this out with your local council. The rules will be particularly strict if you live in a conservation area. Your house and even your out-buildings may be 'listed'. A Devonshire farmer recently found that his four-holer outside privy had been listed, so be warned. Nothing may be added or subtracted to or from a listed building, and even repairs must be to an agreed standard. Do not be tempted to go ahead and hope to 'get away with it'. The odds are that you will not. As well as being fined quite heavily, you may well be made to rebuild or pull down an unauthorised alteration, and will earn the opprobrium of all and sundry.

Your neighbours will have desires, some of them legally enforce-able, to light, privacy and, in some cases, rights-of-way or common access over your land which must not be obstructed, restricted or altered without prior arrangement. If this irritates you, just im-agine how you would feel if the position was reversed. Whenever possible, establish friendly relations with all your neighbours and sort things out with them well in advance.

Any lawyer will tell you of the horrors, frustrations and wildly escalating costs of disputes between neighbours. Even if right is on your side, you will need a first-class legal adviser and a full purse to establish the facts. Whichever way the verdict goes, much bitterness will remain—sometimes for years.

Trees are quite frequently covered by a preservation order and, once again, in conservation areas, all the trees may be protected. You must get permission before you cut them down or carry out any serious pruning. If the trees are diseased and likely to drop on your head at the first puff of wind, you may be able to get them cut down, and if they are of any size at all, get the help of a good tree surgeon. He will be able to tell you if all or part of the tree could be saved, and this is no time for false economies. One hefty tree-trunk plummeting down in an uncontrolled fashion, can cause a truly horrendous amount of damage, as well as being quite likely to crush your house and your nearest and dearest.

Trees arouse great passions in many people, so that any covert action you take is bound to be noted and reported upon by incensed conservationists (rightly so). Remember that, if the trees are not protected, your neighbour will be entitled to cut back to the boundary the branches of any of your trees that overhang his land, although he must offer the prunings back to you. He must also carry out the pruning without causing damage to the health of the tree. Of course, all this applies equally but in reverse, to any of his trees that may encroach on your land, and the whole process can lead to quite a brisk little exchange of mangled blossom, wasp-eaten plums and chit-chat on the state of the nation.

Remember, too, that if you plant a tree of such vigour and enthusiasm that its roots seek out and cause damage to your neighbour's property, whether it be to his house, outbuildings, walls or drains, you will be held legally liable. Poplars are notorious for causing this kind of damage, and should be planted, as I mentioned before, not less than about 45m (150ft) from all buildings and drains. However, if your neighbour is foolish enough to build over existing roots, even if they do come from your trees, the odds are that you will not be held liable.

Boundary disputes are distressingly common. On some deeds it is made quite clear whose fence or wall is whose, and then the owner can be made responsible for its upkeep and repair, in theory at least. However, in many cases, the ownership is not clear, and then it will make sense for both parties to share all expenses as this will be of benefit to both, although they may not be too keen to chip in for your fancier flights of *treillage,* and if your neighbours are impoverished pensioners or permanently stoned refugees from the Peace convoy, you may have to grit your teeth and pay for the lot. This will still be worth doing and will probably save you money in the long run, by keeping your own children, pets and elderly dependants in, while, with any luck, repelling those belonging to others, as well as making life more difficult for the local villains.

Incidentally, one is considered to be responsible for the actions of one's dogs but not one's cats, which is probably just as well for the cats. You are not allowed to take pot shots at trespassing pussies, but you might get away with water-pistols. In theory, keeping a dog will scare off the cats, but in practice I find that the cats sit on the wall and jeer at my dog, which rouses him to such a pitch of impotent fury that he crashes about the garden in a fruitless attempt to get at them, thereby causing more damage than twenty cats.

It is as well to make sure that your household insurance policy covers you for accidental injury on your property, such as falls caused by faulty surfaces or knock-out blows from falling slates and expiring elms. You will be liable for any damage that you or your contractors cause to your neighbour's property, to the main services such as water, gas, electricity and drains, and to telephone and cable TV lines. In fact, when you engage a contractor it is as well to make sure that he is suitably insured; get it confirmed in writing and, if in doubt, ask to see his policy. Remember that if your property is rented or leasehold, the landlord or freeholder may well have included restrictive clauses in the lease which can, in extreme cases, even apply to the colour of the paintwork on the house; so, once again, check up.

Finally, all surplus water on your land should drain away within your boundaries or into your drainage system. It should not be discharged onto your neighbour's property or onto the public highway.

3   DIRT CHEAP

Material savings

With all the research and planning done, it is time to think of construction and to find the necessary materials. Many of these may be already on site, but in disguise. The ruined air-raid shelter and the pile of builder's rubble by the back door can provide bricks for walls and hardcore for paths and terraces. Earth excavated to make a pool or lay drains can be used in raised beds or to change levels. If you are making a sunken garden, the earth removed can be spread over the raised area to double the depth in half the time.

If you get the go-ahead to cut down a tree, slices from the trunk can be used as an informal woodland path or as 'stepping stones'. Straight branches, cut into varying lengths and trimmed, will make stakes for trees and shrubs. Cut into even shorter lengths, about 45 to 60cm (18" to 2ft), they can be hammered into the ground to make an informal retaining 'wall' for a raised bed or banks. In a cottage garden, the smaller branches can be used for 'rustic' screens, fences and arches. The twiggy branches will make poles for peas and beans, provide unobtrusive support for straggling plants and can be placed as a small protective circle round frail young plants to give them a chance to get established and to prevent accidental damage. The trimmings of prickly shrubs, such as Berberis, Gorse and Holly, can be used to repel cats (see Chapter 11).

It is quite usual to find old cinders and clinkers when digging over neglected gardens. These are left over from the days of solid-fuel fires and boilers. Save the large clinkers for hardcore and the cinders to make a *cordon sanitaire* round young plants that the slugs might fancy.

Fat sections of the tree trunk, cut into short lengths, can make the supports for an informal seat which can be made from an old plank, an oblong of paving, (either stone or concrete) or perhaps the marble top of an old washstand. These turn up surprisingly often in gardens. Usually they are chipped or broken, in which case you can cut them into smaller pieces and use them for shelves or pastry boards. Nothing to do with gardening, I know, but I throw in the hint for good measure. If they are large and unbroken they will make a splendid top for a garden table, as will those large slabs of slate that were used to roof the outside privy. Slate slabs can also

make a handsome centre to a paved area or a useful roof to the
dustbin hide. A stone cutter can be hired quite easily.

Almost anything can be used to make paths and terraces. In large
areas, a mixture of materials can be very effective, if carefully
designed. Round up all the odd bricks, quarry tiles, bits and pieces
of stone and slate, cobbles, flints, pebbles, and gravel that you can
lay your hands on, as well as wooden battens, sliced tree-trunk and
old railway sleepers. All can be pressed into service in some way or
other. If there is not enough material in your garden, search
through skips, the council tip and odd corners of builders' yards
and demolition sites. Roofing slates can be used to retain soil or to
make a damp-proof course when planting beds are made along the
walls of the house.

Builders, electricians and plumbers will leave all sorts of useful
odds and ends behind them. Lengths of white flex or bell-wire can
be stretched between wall nails as plant supports on a white wall,
black or brown flex on brick walls. Lengths and off-cuts of wood
can be used for a wide range of garden projects—containers,
fencing, trellises, summerhouses and far pavilions. Old floor-
boards will make a robust tree-house. Pieces of 5×2.5cm ($2'' \times 1''$)
timber, treated with preservative, would make a strong 'decking'
over a tatty bit of terrace or roof garden (see pp. 73–5 and Chapter
9). Even the flimsiest of battens (such as those used in the old
lath-and-plaster ceilings, which are often found piled into skips
when houses are being gutted) can be used to make a lightweight
trellis for decorative purposes only, or to support one of the more
delicate annual climbers (Morning Glories or Black-eyed-Susans;
anything more thug-like would destroy it).

Bits of plastic plumbing can be used for water gardening, if well
hidden by lush planting, while stripped-out iron piping will make
very strong supports for all sorts of plants. Plastic sheeting could be
used to make a garden pool; it might not last for ever but would
serve for a while. It would also do duty as a cheap and quickly
dismantled paddling pool, or as a lining to all sorts of improvised
containers (remember to punch some drainage holes or the plants

will drown in wet weather or from over-watering). Plastic sheeting can be used under areas of paving and gravel, to suppress weeds, and black plastic can be laid between newly-planted shrubs to keep the weeds down while the shrubs get established. Hold the plastic down with bricks or stones. Builder's sacks, cut open at both ends, can be used round a twig frame, as a wind-break or frost guard, popped over a frail plant. Use these sacks to store compost and fallen leaves so that they can rot down in odourless comfort.

Chimney pots, clay or earthenware drain-pipes, disused sinks and lavatories can all be used as containers. Galvanised water-tanks make capacious and handsome planting bays. Raise them up on a few bricks, to help drainage, and paint them to match the walls or woodwork. This is probably the cheapest way to grow a tree, large shrub or vigorous climber in a container, as they will hold the amount of soil needed to provide the plant with a good root system. Old tin trunks, ammunition boxes, baths and large barrels are other possibilities.

Do not be tempted to use left-over heaps of builder's sand for the children's sandpit. It will stain their clothes a nasty dingy yellow. Silver sand is the one for this job. Use the builder's sand to spread over hardcore, under paths and terraces, or to line the garden pool to make a smooth base for the plastic liner. Half-bags of cement are often left behind and, if these have not 'gone off', use them to make a mortar for walls and terraces. If they have gone off, use the lumps for hardcore. During the war, sacks of cement mix were piled up to make road blocks. They hardened off beautifully and, when the sacks rotted away, where often white-washed. This would be one way to construct walls in utility areas. Odds and ends of paint can be used to paint walls, containers and woodwork. Use Universal Stainers to shade them the colours you need.

Having used up all the bits and pieces that are lying around the house and garden, turn your eyes further afield. As I have said before, skips and tips are the obvious places to start. Ask the builders or the council workmen, if they are about, for permission before carting off your 'find'. The most likely discoveries will be soil, bricks, timber and containers of all sorts, but in time you may find turf, tiles, paving, statues, garden furniture and every kind of plant from trees to Water-lilies. Many houses that were built before the First World War had floors of York stone, especially in cellars and basements. These are still being broken up and thrown into skips so that a concrete screed can be laid over a d.p.c. If you see a house that is being gutted, talk nicely to the workmen and, for a few pounds, they may well dig up the slabs unbroken and load them into your boot. Do not take too many at a time or they will wreck your car, which will not be much of an economy. The men will usually agree to save them for your next trip. If they have thrown the broken pieces in the skip, fish them out and either use them as crazy paving or stepping stones in the lawn and flower border, or hire the stone cutter and trim them into regular shapes for steps, coping or paving. Some councils have old paving stones or granite setts to sell, but more often they sell them in bulk to large garden centres where you can buy them at a price.

Demolition sites and yards are good hunting grounds for construction materials, if you can get there before everything is burnt or carted off to be dumped. Firms specialising in 'Architectural Salvage', that is bits and pieces from such sites, are springing up all over the place and are worth searching out. Of course, things will be more expensive there than 'buying a drink' for the demolition gang, but still a good buy.

For ornamental items and containers, auctions (especially in bad weather), jumble sales, church and village fêtes (the white elephant stall) and car boot sales are the places to look, if you cannot find what you want in the skip. Scrap-metal yards are worth visiting if you want gates, railings and balconies, amongst other things, while postcards in the local shop and small ads in *Exchange and Mart* or the local papers will reveal endless bargains. Only the other day I read an advertisement for 100 palm trees, which were surplus to a film company's requirements. These would have been just the thing for a garden with a tropical theme. *Exchange and Mart* comes out on Thursdays and has thousands of avid readers, so you need to be quick off the mark to get anything. If you live in the country, you may find exactly what you need in hedgerows and ditches, while town-dwellers find the most amazing things abandoned on the pavements.

Country friends may well be able to provide you with small quantities of soil and turf, manure, perhaps, and seedling trees. Most gardening friends will be only too happy to swap seeds, seedlings, cuttings and thinnings with you. While some gardeners are like cooks who refuse to part with their recipes (which they probably pinched from someone else anyway), others, the majority in fact, are a generous, open-handed lot, who will share both their experience and their treasures with you, so your best plan is to cultivate the company of as many of them as possible, and, indeed, this is often the only way to obtain some of the more unusual plants.

Any plant that you cannot scrounge from others or propagate yourself will have to be paid for. Look out for end-of-season bargains, stock from nurseries which are closing down or moving, and for special offers in the national, local and gardening press, although these should be treated with a certain amount of caution, especially those which offer dashingly-named plants that you cannot trace in catalogues or reference books. Be particularly suspicious of those plants guaranteed to grow a mile-a-minute and astonish your friends with a million blooms; these will probably strangle your children and impale the postman, being, as likely as not, a Russian Vine or a remarkably vicious hedging rose. There *are* bargains to be found at the garden centres, either deliberate loss-leaders or inhabitants of the casualty ward—a trolley where some dejected-looking plants that have lost their get-up-and-go for some reason, huddle together under a sign saying, 'Everything here 70p'. Why is it always 70p, I wonder? Have you noticed? Why not 60p or 25? It is worth considering these pathetic creatures; quite often they will respond to a little attention (don't we all?) and will reward you by perking up and making a quick recovery, or at least a reasonable amount of growth next season. Other garden centres are even more ruthless and chuck out plants that are merely less than perfect. It is worth peering into their rubbish bins, whilst whistling casually and pretending that your eye just alighted there by chance as you strolled by. Florists, too, can be rather reckless at the end of the day, so have a quick gander there as well.

If you are one of nature's organisers, you could set up a local gardener's club or horticultural society. These can often negotiate very favourable terms with nurserymen and suppliers for bulk purchases. At the very least, you would be able to share carriage charges. As a lone hunter, you can haunt the plant stalls of markets, jumbles, coffee mornings, fêtes, fairs and bazaars. Mostly you will find mildewed Michaelmas Daisies, laced with couch-grass, but the most surprising treasures can turn up. Firms that mount exhibits at flower and horticultural shows often sell off the plants at the end of the show for reduced prices, while some of them have a sidestall, selling small plants for—you've guessed it—70p. It is always worth looking in Woolies or the other chain stores, while gardens that are open to the public, from the grandest to the most humble, will often sell a few plants, some of which may be very desirable, and others run a flourishing nursery business on the side.

Do not be tempted to dig up plants from the countryside. Almost all land belongs to somebody and most of our wild plants are protected by law. However, there are several firms that sell wild flower seeds, and this would be a cheap way to fill a wild or cottage garden. It is not a good idea to bring back plants from your trips abroad; you may well bring back more than you bargained for in the way of pests and diseases, and the customs officers will not be amused. If you are a serious and knowledgeable plant collector, you will know about the necessary licences to import plants and seeds, etc.

It would be wise to consult local by-laws before helping yourself to large pebbles, stones and chunks of rock from country or seaside, but it is safe to collect driftwood and those wonderfully gnarled and knotted roots that are washed up from time to time.

Tropical shells can be picked up quite cheaply at junk shops and jumble sales: they look good in cottage gardens, as do scallop shells, which you can buy for a few pennies at the fishmonger's. They make a charming edge to a child's garden ('Mary, Mary, quite contrary . . .'). Of course, if you eat a lot of scallops, the shells will come free.

Lawns can be grown quite cheaply from seed, if you do all the necessary levelling and preparation yourself. Make sure that you get good quality seed and choose one that is suitable for your soil, etc. Special mixtures can be obtained for growing under trees, for heavy duty and other specialist needs. For a small to medium-sized lawn, turf is not that expensive, and often the delivery charge is

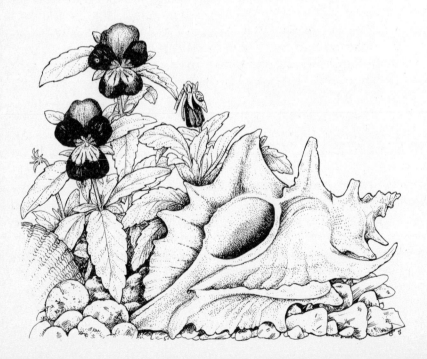

more than the price of the turf, so bigger lawns are not *that* much more expensive than tiny ones. Whether you seed or turf, invest in some kind of water sprinkler or your beautiful greensward may shrivel up in the first hot spell. A better idea, however, is to renovate the existing grass, by a sustained campaign of cutting, feeding, spiking and weeding, as described in Chapter 4. Even the most unpromising and dog-eared turf will respond to this kind of care.

If you decide to grub up an old lawn, do not throw out the turves. Stack them away somewhere in a quiet corner to rot down to a rich compost or place them at the bottom of the trench when digging over the flower and vegetable beds. Roses love to be planted over chopped-up turves, and it is a good idea to put a layer of turf, upside-down, over the drainage crocks at the bottom of plant containers, to prevent the planting medium being washed away and to give the plants a healthy boost as it rots down.

If your soil is very stony, save any stones that you have raked up and use them to improve drainage in damp areas, or to crock up a container, or as hardcore for paths and terraces. I had an uncle who ran a prep school. He and his wife were fanatical gardeners. Every day, a crocodile of small boys was taken for a walk along the roads surrounding the school. Each lad was instructed to fill his pockets with shale and gravel from those heaps that the council had prudently placed beside the road for repairs and gritting. On their return for tea, all pockets were turned out and the spoils used to top-dress the rockeries and alpine beds. This was economy at an inspirational level and a fine lesson in the entrepreneurial virtues.

Container gardening on the cheap will develop your constructional skills and a good eye for a potential pot. In the cottage garden almost anything can be pressed into service: barrels, of course, and old sinks; lavatories frothing over with Ivy and Nasturtiums; buckets, hip-baths and chamber-pots, pots, pans, jars and crocks, fire grates and rubber tyres—anything goes. Things are rather different in a formal setting. This is where the water tank will come into its own. Painted a matt greenish-black, it will look remarkably like an antique lead cistern. Here, too, you may make neat beds of bricks, rescued from the skip, to match the brickwork of the house, or painted to match the walls and woodwork. Breeze-blocks make a good, strong wall or raised bed; not the most elegant solution, perhaps, but again, paint them to match the rest of the place, and cover them with neat trellis, painted the same or in contrast. Fix a coping along the top, unless you plan to plant the edges with Ivy or some other sprawling plant, and the effect will be quite solid and imposing. Clay pots will suit almost all schemes and, if you stick to plain, machine-made pots, are not very expensive. One large enough to take a small tree will cost about as much as a bottle of supermarket gin, and the pleasure it will bring will last considerably longer.

Once you splurge out upon imported, hand-thrown pots, you are into big money, but if you have room for just one, the outlay would be justified by the impact. If there is a small pottery in your part of the world, try and persuade them to sell you their 'seconds' —those that have small cracks and chips or those that have gone wrong in the kiln. All sorts of glazed pots can be used, but you must make drainage holes, using a masonry bit with your drill. Keep a look-out in builders' yards for attractive chimney pots, as these come in many traditional designs and colours. Old ones are getting quite expensive now but can be picked up occasionally. Even sections of large concrete drainpipe can be used in a modern setting. Old coppers and boilers, as well as all sorts of metal containers, can be used. They, too, must have drainage holes drilled into them and it is a good idea to paint them on the inside as some metals are toxic to plants.

Wooden window-boxes, planters and square Versailles 'caisses' can be made from old floor-boards, and off-cuts of timber. Roof timbers will make splendid pergolas. All wood should be treated with a non-toxic wood preservative or painted, both inside and out, and the containers should be raised clear of the ground on runners or bricks to avoid rotting.

It will probably be necessary to improve the soil in all or in part of your garden. Compost heaps provide the cheapest improver of all, so start a compost heap right away. If you have the room, allow for two or three, on the principle of 'one on, one off and one in the drawer'. Where space is limited, there are many neat containers of wood, metal or plastic to keep things under control and speed up the process. An old dustbin with the base knocked out and air holes punched in round the bottom edge will do the job quite well and so will black plastic sacks, as discussed in Chapter 2. This is a good way to deal with fallen leaves. They take longer to rot down than garden and kitchen waste, so should be bagged up separately and left for two years when they will have become splendid leaf mould. Do not add the leaves from Plane trees or conifer needles. These should be put on the bonfire and the ashes added to the compost heap.

In the Autumn, I make forays into the countryside, armed with black bags and two boards. I find a quiet place where the road runs through beech or oak woods and just grab up boardfuls of fallen leaves from the roadside, to the acute embarrassment of my children. I do the same with horse-droppings and sometimes wonder if this was a contributory factor in my divorce. If visiting stable or farm owning friends, always go armed with shovel and sacks. Try and get the oldest, well-rotted manure, as this can be spread around straight away. Fresh manure can be added in small doses to the compost heap, to act as an accelerator, and so can the dog faeces that you have scooped up from the lawn.

If you have a large garden, it might be worth investing in one of the compost-shredding machines, or an old chaff-cutter (keep both well away from all children). These chomp everything down to a fine mince which will rot away very quickly and could be applied as a mulch right away. Never add perennial weeds or diseased plants to the compost heap; burn them instead. Bracken could be processed in the cutter and fed to your Lilies which would be grateful. It can also be put into a bucket and chopped up with the garden shears, to be added to the heap or spread as a protective mulch above any delicate favourites. Seaweed can be used in the same way; it can also be dug into the bottom spit of soil when trenching or spread over the top to rot down, but this is rather smelly (however, see Chapter 6, p. 120).

Finally, to the equipment and tools you will need. I have already cited private auctions as a fertile hunting ground for good, cheap tools, but if you have moved into an old house, you may well find an abandoned cache of perfectly usable if venerable tools in the garden shed or air-raid shelter. Even those that are broken can often be mended, and if it is only a matter of replacing the handle, you can do that yourself with a piece of broom handle and a nail or Araldite.

Good solid tools are a sound investment, but don't think you have to buy everything in stainless steel, and only buy those you really need (a rake will be of little use in a paved courtyard). In general, it is surprising how little you can make do with if you can only afford the basic essentials.

4 SPADEWORK

Construction and landscaping

Now comes the back-breaking bit, if you are starting from scratch. For those lucky enough to have a garden that is already in good shape and to their liking, there will probably be only the odd spot demanding construction techniques, but for many others, who are facing a new or badly neglected and derelict plot, there is hard work ahead.

It may sound rather obvious, but first attend to your entrance and exits. In larger gardens it will be helpful to have an entrance large enough to admit a small lorry, or at least a van, for receiving loads of material—turf, gravel, manure, etc., all of which come a lot cheaper by the lorry-load—and to allow machinery such as a cultivator or a cement-mixer into the place. Of course, this is a policy of perfection; many of us will have to cart everything through the house to the detriment of carpets, wallpaper and relationships.

If your garden has no access other than through the house, do try and get the worst of the debris out, and the bulk of construction materials and the larger plants, such as shrubs and trees, into the garden before you move in, or at least before the carpets are down. When this is not possible, it will be worth investing in some of the tough strips of plastic carpet protector if you have much work to be carried out. For smaller, cleaner, projects, dust sheets or old newspaper can help to protect from the worst of the mess. No matter how careful you and your gang are, there will most certainly be some accident or other; someone trips and drops an armful of rubbish, a bag of cement splits as you are carrying it, or a plant container falls off the plant, scattering soil and perhaps muddy water over a horribly wide area, so that all the protective care you take will be well worth while.

In front gardens, it will be worth preserving or copying the original gate, if you are lucky enough to have one. If yours has gone missing, see if any of your neighbours has still got one that you can copy. This may not be exactly cheap, if the gate is ironwork, but it will add such style to the place that you may well have to do little else, and it *will* keep out those dogs whose horrid owners turn them loose. If the gate was a wooden one, you may be able to copy it yourself, or at least get a local carpenter to do it for you. Whichever, some of the expense will be defrayed by the cost of the plants that will be saved from the dogs. Whatever gate you choose should be in sympathy with the house; simple picket-style for a cottage, or dignified iron for a period town house, and plain and sturdy for a modern building.

This rule applies to your boundaries, too. If you are exceptionally lucky, you may have good, sound walls around your property or a well-grown and maintained hedge or fence. If they are mostly in good order, with just one or two dodgy patches, then these can usually be repaired. All too often, however, the boundaries are missing or in disrepair. In this case, they should be your first priority. I cannot pretend that to reinstate a wall can ever be an economical practice, but shaky ones can be shored up with buttresses, and gaps can be rebuilt. That is something you could probably do yourself with the aid of a book or by watching bricklayers at work . . . In fact it is a splendid policy to watch any tradesman you come across, whether bricklayer, plasterer, carpenter or whatever, as it is infinitely easier to follow printed instructions if you have seen someone carry out similar work. In most cases, they will be only too pleased to give you helpful advice, if you choose your time carefully and do not interrupt them at a critical moment.

Bricks can be 'stretched', of course, by laying in open or honeycomb courses, but this is more suitable for a low front wall or for internal screening, than for a boundary; you could, however, add a

WALLS

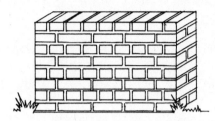

English bond

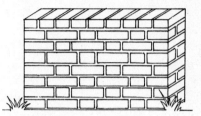

Flemish bond

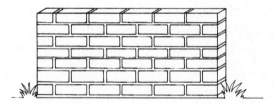

Stretcher bond

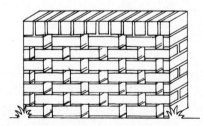

Honeycomb 1

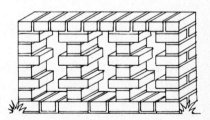

Honeycomb 2

section of honeycomb walling to the top of your brick wall, which would give a rather nice, airy feeling and make the bricks go further.

Concrete blocks are much cheaper than bricks, and far quicker to lay, but they are not, in themselves, possessed of immediate allure. However, for a strong wall they can be faced with brick, which would be more economical than a double brick wall, or they may be rendered and painted. I have seen them un-rendered and painted a dark green, which really looked rather elegant. A dark green trellis had been placed in front of the blocks, and a wooden coping added, but you could use a concrete tile or reconstituted stone coping if you wished. You could try other colours: white or black, terracotta, primrose yellow, dark blue, or that weathered, faded blue-green which is so popular for garden furniture. The trellis could be matching or contrasting, and if you made the whole thing yourself, could hardly be more cost-effective, especially if you have 'liberated' the materials.

If you live in areas where natural stone is abundant, you may be lucky enough to have stone walls. They are usually very strong but, nowadays, they are not cheap to repair or to build from scratch, so if yours has gaps, find someone to repair at least a section of it and watch them carefully so that you can do the job yourself next time.

Fencing, too, can be repaired and patched in some cases. If the supports are a bit rocky, there are various methods of strengthening them, such as inserting them into metal sockets, bolting them to concrete spurs, or buttressing them with sound timber. Even an old piece of angle-iron will help. These measures are quite good for prolonging the life of a fence if the panels are sound, and only the base of the uprights have become rotten. If all the fencing is ropy, it will be better to renew it right away, rather than wait for a year or two and risk the expensive damage which will probably be inflicted on the plants you have so carefully established. If you decide to do the job yourself, measure up carefully to avoid wastage and, if possible, use the best quality timber, whether bought or 'found', as

TRELLIS

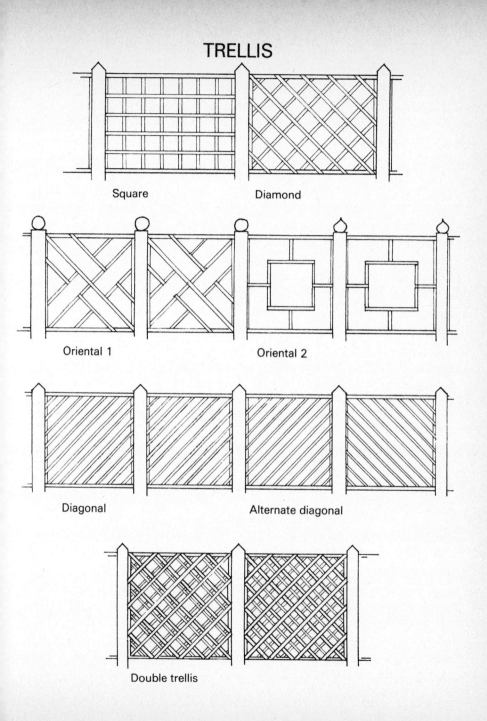

Square

Diamond

Oriental 1

Oriental 2

Diagonal

Alternate diagonal

Double trellis

this will prove to be the most economical method in the long run. If you prefer to have a local handyman or fencing contractor to do the work for you, make careful enquiries among the neighbours and, if possible, try to see some work that they have carried out, before giving them the job; get several estimates, too.

There are various types of fencing. The most commonly used are overlap fencing (in which the laps may be either horizontal or vertical); interwoven panels, including panels which incorporate a section of trellis at the top; picket fencing (which you could make yourself), chestnut paling and wattle hurdles. These last two look good in an informal or rural setting but are not very long lasting. They are, however, ideal in temporary situations, and odd panels can be used to protect vulnerable young plants from the prevailing winds, thus giving them a chance to get their toes dug in and gain some strength.

Then there are post and rail fencing, (which can be of various designs, from the plainest two-rails-to-a-post variety to elaborate Chinoiserie); ranch fencing (which can be open- or close-boarded, and which will suit the more modern property); as well as rustic fencing which is really only suitable for a very informal setting, such as a cottage garden, perhaps.

You may well be able to find the timber for these wooden fences on skips and demolition sites. Picket and ranch-type fencing will usually look best when painted, but remember that those portions of the uprights which are below ground should be treated with a wood preservative, such as Cuprinol or creosote. Your wooden fencing will last longer if you give it a coping and caps for the uprights, plus a gravel board along the base, to save the actual fencing from rot.

If you are not going to paint your wooden fencing, it should be treated with preservative, but do not use creosote on wood which is going to be in contact with living plants, as it is toxic to them. In these cases, use a non-toxic preservative; your local hardware shop or garden centre will advise you, and the preservative comes in various colours, the most commonly available being

FENCING

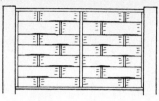

Interwoven

Overlap

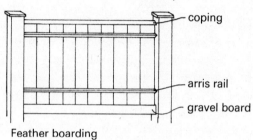

coping

arris rail

gravel board

Feather boarding

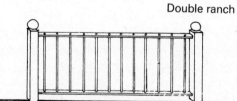

Picket fence

Ranch

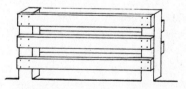

Double ranch

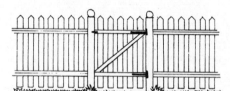

Imitation iron railings
made from battens and dowelling
painted with black gloss

brown or dark green, which can look very handsome in the right place.

You may have, or wish to have, iron railings. It is sometimes possible to buy these or to match up missing sections of existing railings by scouting round the scrap metal yards or the local Architectural Salvage shops. For a larger outlay, a blacksmith will copy most patterns for you.

At the bottom end of the scale come posts and wire or chain-link fencing. Nobody can pretend that they are things of beauty, but they can provide a good temporary solution, to protect a young hedge, or, more permanently, a support for an evergreen climber, like Honeysuckle 'Halliana', or Ivy. They are worth considering when money is short, or your stay temporary, and the Honeysuckle will give you the added advantage of flowers and scent.

If you are going for a hedge, consider carefully the pros and cons of the different hedging plants before you buy. Make sure that the plants are suitable for your soil and conditions. If you have a large garden and want a reasonably tall hedge, *Cupressocyparis leylandii* is probably your best bet, as it is about the fastest growing sturdy conifer. It also has an attractive golden form, 'Castlewellan'. You can often find these two on offer in the gardening press and, so long as you choose a reputable supplier, this is a good way to buy. There are other good choices for hedging which I shall discuss later in Chapter 6.

The advantage of a hedge, especially a well maintained evergreen hedge, (and I suppose that Yew is the noblest of them all) is that it provides such a handsome backdrop for the rest of the garden, as well as privacy, and, if well sited, a useful windbreak; although staggered planting, rather than a solid wodge, is better for that. It is important to plant them out at a reasonable distance apart, from about 30cm (12") for smaller, slow-growing subjects, to 90cm (3') for vigorous, fast-growing *leylandii*.

Whatever you choose for your boundaries, *do* remember to leave an exit; we had a saintly but rather simple gardener when I was a child, who constructed a beautifully efficient fence, while his small son tugged at his sleeves, whining, 'Dad, Dad, how do we get out, Dad . . . ?' There they were, father, son and barrow-load of wood, completely enclosed.

If you really cannot afford to mend the boundaries with the appropriate materials, or are staying such a short time that expensive repairs are not worth while, stretch barbed wire across the gap to repel intruders and then plant in front of it the largest, cheapest evergreen that you can find. Alternatively, if you have a little artistic talent, fix some off-cuts of wood across the gap and paint them to match the surrounding boundary. A bit of artful planting in front of this, or a quick-growing climber trailing across it, will help it to blend in neatly.

If time is not a matter of urgency, take your own cuttings to make the cheapest boundary hedge of all. Of course, you will have to give it some protection with wire or stakes until it is strong enough to stand up for itself. If you live in the country, you may be able to find enough seedling plants to dig up and replant in well-prepared land, but be sure to ask the owners of the land first, and you will have to be patient. Your hedge will take some years to look anything at all.

Having attended to the exits, entrances and boundaries, now is the time to consider any extra protection from the prevailing winds. This will be particularly important if you are near the sea, as the winds will carry salt for about five miles inland, and this can be very destructive to many plants. It is a common mistake to plant solid belts of trees and shrubs, for these have exactly the opposite effect to that which was intended. The frustrated wind comes hurtling over them and thumps down on the other side in a whirl of turbulence which can cause havoc. To a certain extent, in larger gardens, this effect can be alleviated by allowing the planting to rise gradually from the upwind side to its maximum height. In smaller places, staggered planting or pierced screening, rather than a sheer mass, is more effective. You could construct a small sloping mound and plant your shelter on this to gain some instant height.

If your garden is uniformly flat, you may find it worth while to change the levels, or, if the existing slopes are very steep, some levelling and terracing may be necessary. The usual method is called 'cut and fill'. This consists of cutting into the slope, moving the topsoil and placing it to one side in small heaps so that it does not become consolidated, then levelling off the subsoil by removing it from the upper part of the slope and using it to build up the lower part. Then the topsoil is replaced. These raised areas will usually need some kind of retaining wall to keep them intact, although if they are allowed to run off into a gentle slope, the earth may be retained by turfing, sowing grass-seed or planting ground-cover.

For earth-mowing over larger areas, it may be necessary to bring in contractors but, once again, before entrusting them with the job make sure that they are a well-established outfit and have been recommended to you by others. Make sure, too, that you are around while they 'gyre and gimble in the wabe' or the result may be a lot less frabjous than you had hoped. Give a man an earth mover, and he seldom knows when to stop . . . trees, shrubs, glades and rosebeds will all disappear into his maw. They are also

CUT AND FILL

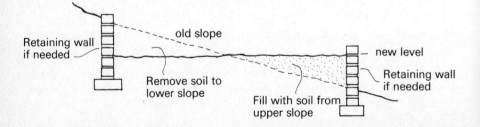

quite keen on leaving mounds of earth where you least expect or want them, claiming that they thought you would like to make a nice rockery there, and can turn rather huffy when you deny this hotly.

With the initial 'sculpting' of the garden done, it will be time to lay on any necessary services—the drains if necessary, water supplies and electricity. That done, you will have to make your hard surfaces, the paths, terraces and the bases for outbuildings, etc. Every material has its advantages and disadvantages. Stone is expensive and heavy to handle, and in some conditions it can become slippery. On the other hand, it is immensely handsome, hard-wearing and easily maintained. If you do go for stone, try and keep to one that occurs naturally in your area, although second-hand York paving looks good in most places, having a simplicity that fits in practically anywhere. Similarly, if you are using bricks, it is generally more effective to use those that are the same as, or resemble, those used in the construction of the house: second-hand stocks in London; red bricks for red-brick houses; modern, perhaps engineering bricks for modern properties, etc. Some concrete slabs can look right in modern settings, but I think that, even there, they look more effective if edged with courses of bricks or cobbles.

Gravel (or pea-shingle) is the most adaptable of surfaces, either on its own or combined with others. It is, comparatively, very cheap, easy to lay and, really, pretty easy to maintain: a little raking from time to time, the odd application of weedkiller and an occasional top-dressing to any worn patches. It has the advantage that you can alter its position quite easily, and you can plant through it, too, which can give a romantic air to the whole thing. Many people shudder when I suggest gravel, thinking of those municipal graveyards where the marble-edged plots are filled with chippings, but nothing is more natural-looking or mellow than honey-coloured gravel, edged with billowing plants, and it fits in happily with any period and style of house. If you are afraid that it will cling to your shoes and come into the house, lay a few slabs of stone or a patch of brickwork in front of the door sills, which should take care of the problem. The larger grades of gravel will never stick to your shoes, and a 2cm (¾″) grade has a good, strong 'feel', although you can still stand a table and chairs comfortably upon it.

If the area is to have heavy use, put a 15cm (6″) layer of well-rammed hardcore down first, then a 5–8cm (2″–3″) layer of consolidated hoggin or builder's sand, before adding the gravel in a thin layer of about 2.5–4cm (1″–1½″) and rolling it in. Anything deeper would be difficult to walk on. You can hire a roller and a rammer quite cheaply from tool hire shops. Get a hollow roller that can be filled with water when it is on site, as it is much easier to handle, although not quite so heavy as the solid ones. If the gravel is to be purely ornamental, or in areas of light use, omit the hardcore, especially if you intend to plant through the gravelled surface. Many plants are at their happiest in the good drainage system that gravel provides for them.

I have an ancient gardening manual which recommends adding crushed sea shells to gravel, to prevent it sticking to one's feet, but I have no idea whether this works out or not, nor, if it does, where you could get hold of such stuff. Perhaps you could gather the shells, put them into heavy duty plastic sacks and persuade the local Boy Scouts to jump up and down on them in Bob-a-job week?

Areas of gravel will need some kind of edging to keep them in their place, unless they are in an already contained area, such as a sunken garden. They can be edged with thin strips of treated timber, bricks, concrete or stone curbing, even with scallop shells if you are feeling whimsical, or with barley sugar edging tiles— either the original ones (and I once found a load of these on a council dump) or the copies which are now being made again.

Bricks can be laid on a similar foundation if you are laying them loose. This has several advantages: the layout can be changed easily; odd bricks which crack or flake can be replaced; they will drain quickly and small plants and bulbs can be established between them in informal settings; while an odd application of weedkiller will keep things neat in the more formal setting. Areas of gravel or loose bricks should be slightly cambered to assist drainage.

Where something firmer is required, lay the bricks in a layer of mortar, instead of sand, over the hardcore base. A 5cm (2″) layer of 4 to 1 dry mortar should do the trick. Mix the mortar well and shovel it onto the area to be paved. Pulling a piece of board from one end to the other will help you to level it. Brush more of the same dry mix between the bricks when they are laid and the natural dampness in the soil and in the atmosphere will cause both the bedding mortar and the pointing to 'go off' slowly and make a firm surface, without the risk of staining that comes from using a wet mix. In very dry weather, sprinkle gently with water after laying. Paths and terraces laid in this firm fashion will need to have a very slight tilt to carry off surface water to some form of drainage away from the house—into the grass or beds in 'soft' areas, or into gullies, drain-traps or soak-aways in 'hard' areas. Without this drainage, the surfaces can become slimy with algae or treacherous with ice in bad weather. A fall of about 2.5cm (1″) in two yards should be about right.

If you are laying a very small area of brick, it would be easier to use a bag or two of ready-mix sand-and-cement. This is also the answer where you are working in an area which is hard to get at, or where access is through the house, but it is quite a bit more expensive than making your own mix. Whichever you use, put some form of protection down before you mix up, to prevent staining. Plastic sheeting or off-cuts of chipboard or hardboard will do.

One easy way to get a smooth, regular surface and a continuous tilt, is to drive small pegs into the ground on each side of the area, marking the top and bottom of the slope. A straight piece of timber is then placed along this row of pegs at the desired level of the finished surface, and another board, placed across them and checked with a spirit level, can be moved down the slope as you work, ensuring that you are keeping to a smooth fall.

In theory, you should use specially hardened bricks, paviors or engineering bricks for a durable surface, but in practice, gather your bricks where ye may; most of them will last a reasonable time and those that do crumble can be prised-out and replaced. Second-hand bricks have a pleasant, lived-in look which seems happily at home in most settings.

There is a variety of patterns in which they can be laid. Straight courses, walling bonds, basket weave and herringbone are the easiest to do, although the latter will need some cutting for alternate courses at the edge, but you can overcome the necessity for this by leaving the edges jagged, laying a straight course of bricks along each side and infilling the gaps with gravel. In fact, it always looks neat to finish off areas of brickwork with a course or two of straight bricks, either side by side or head on. The larger the area of brickwork, the simpler the pattern should be, or the effect will be turbulent rather than soothing; in small areas, however, your imagination can run riot, with squares, circles, triangles and stars. The bricks can be laid on edge, with their flat surfaces uppermost, or in a mix of both. They are not difficult to cut in half: just chase a line across them, then place a bolster on this groove and give it a sharp tap with a club hammer. Any jagged bits can then be chipped off. Alternatively, as in the herringbone edging, any odd gaps in your pattern can be infilled with gravel, shingle, pebbles, cobbles, small shells or low-growing plants.

Pebbles and cobbles can also be used for paving, either laid loose or set in a mortar bed. Large, rounded pebbles and cobbles set on end, like eggs in a box, are good for areas in which you want to deter walkers, whilst laid on their side, with the flattest surface uppermost, and well bedded down in sand or a mortar-mix, they can be walked on with ease, except perhaps by those with bare feet or stiletto heels.

Quarry tiles and stable tiles also make good paving material for small areas and, like the cobbles, should be set in a layer of dry sand and cement mix (3 to 1) over an 8cm (3″) layer of consolidated hardcore, with more of the same mix brushed between them.

BRICK PAVING

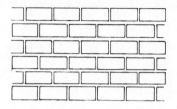

Wall bond

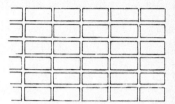

Straight courses

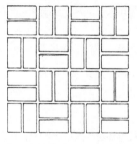

Basketweave —
flat faced

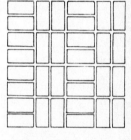

Basketweave —
on edge

Alternate straight
courses

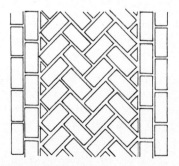

Herringbone 1

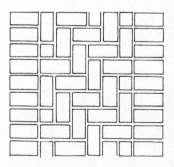

Herringbone 2

PAVING PATTERNS

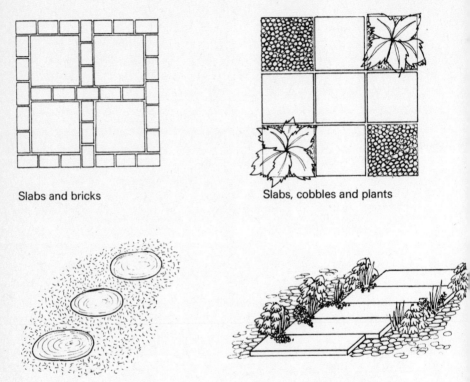

Slabs and bricks

Slabs, cobbles and plants

Wood in bark or gravel

Sleepers, cobbles and plants

Granite setts are laid in the same way over a 10cm (4″) hardcore base.

Stone, reconstituted stone and concrete slabs are probably the easiest to lay (apart from their weight), but the first two are not cheap, unless you have salvaged them from somewhere or other. Concrete slabs are cheap enough, but rather unendearing unless very skilfully sited. The best of them can look right in a modern setting, and the others will do at a pinch for 'utility' areas, but avoid, at all cost, multi-coloured slabs. For areas of very heavy, perhaps vehicular use, they should be set over a poured concrete base. For medium wear, a 5cm (2") bed of sand over a 10cm (4") hardcore base will be the answer and for light use on well drained areas, the heavier slabs can be set on sand laid over compacted soil. A dab of mortar set at each corner and in the middle of the underside of each slab will be a help in getting them level, as they can be tapped down and checked with a spirit level. They can be close-butted or pointed with a dry mortar mix.

You can, of course, use poured concrete for terraces and paths by ordering a load of ready-mix, if you have access to barrow the horrible stuff into your garden, or by getting a hired concrete mixer in there and mixing it yourself. It is much praised in some circles, but I find it incredibly alienating, no matter how cleverly laid and surfaced. I would only use it as the base for huts, etc., and never where it will be seen, but if it does anything for you, it is a cheap enough solution. I am equally unkeen on random or crazy paving; it is unspeakably awful when made from bits of polished marble in assorted colours, or from broken-up concrete slabs. I can just about bear it, in natural stone, for a cottage garden path. If you do go for it, make sure that it is well laid and firmly bedded, or it will prove a trap for the unwary. I prefer to see these odd pieces of stone set as stepping stones, through gravel or pebbles.

It is possible to terrace small areas with wooden decking. If you can get your timber from skips and demolition sites before it ends up on a great bonfire, it will be quite a cheap solution to uneven ground. The planks of treated wood are nailed down onto a system of beams and joists, like a wooden floor, which must, of course, be set on a firm and level foundation. The planks can be laid in a variety of patterns, either in straight courses or diagonally, using galvanised nails.

Decking makes a good, neat cover for tatty concrete yards, so often found at the back of older, urban properties. These are eyesores, but a bore to dig up, as you never know what you are

DECKING

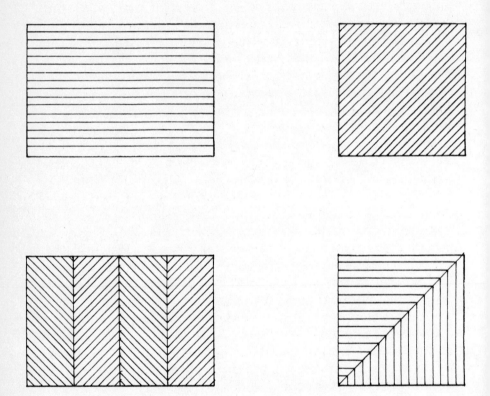

going to disturb—the drains, main services, dead cats, etc. Cover the whole drear, uneven rubble with tidy planks, or lengths of 5 × 2.5 cm (2″ × 1″) timber which you have treated with a suitable wood preservative. Leave a small gap (about 6mm or ¼″) between the planks for drainage. Anything wider could catch narrow heels. A wooden floor can also be made from railway sleepers, and from old beams and slices of tree trunks as well, but all wooden flooring can become slippery in wet weather, so be warned.

Finally, in a wildly informal garden, paths and even small clearings can be surfaced with bark chippings which, like gravel, can be altered easily and planted through. It acts as a weed-suppressing mulch but, unfortunately, birds are enamoured of it and spend happy hours chucking it over their shoulders (do birds have shoulders?) in a most untidy fashion.

Wherever you plan your paths and terraced area, one or more manhole covers are sure to be bang in the middle, where you least want them. It would be expensive to move them but you can usually raise or lower them a little, by the removal or addition of a course or two of bricks, so that the cover will, at least, be flush with its surroundings. It is possible to buy recessed covers which will take slabs, tiles and other surfacing materials. This is splendid if you can fit it in with the general direction of the surfacing, but as often as not the damn' things are set at the weirdest angles so that it is impossible to blend them into any reasonable design. If they are not slap in the middle of a main thoroughfare, immediately in front of a door or in the middle of a narrow path, they can be disguised by a paving slab, some bricks, a container-grown plant or a layer of gravel, all of which can be removed easily enough when necessary. If they are sited where you would inevitably trip over such a disguise, a thin layer of gravel or a neat paint job would be the best you could do.

In anything but the merest courtyard garden, you will probably have some areas of grass. If the existing grass has not been reduced by the builders to charred or muddy wilderness, it can usually be resuscitated by a lot of loving care. Lawns are hard work but, as Nanny used to say, they do pay for dressing. Cut down the jungle-like top growth, mow, and when you can see the whites of the daisies' eyes, start to reclaim the land.

Slice off any hillocks, and fill up any depressions with topsoil. Re-sow both areas. Then it is just a matter of following all the instructions in those depressing 'jobs to be done this month' sections in the gardening articles. After a year of mowing, raking, spiking, feeding, watering, weed-killing and re-sowing failed patches, you should be the exhausted but triumphant owner of a reasonable lawn. If you have to start from scratch, it is obviously cheaper to seed the lawn rather than to turf it, but for smaller areas, the convenience of having an instantly usable lawn may well make it worth the extra expense of turf. The delivery charge is often as much as the price of the turf for small areas, so see if you can share a load with a neighbour and split the cost of the delivery charge between you. For a few square yards of turf, you could collect it yourself in the boot of your car. The turf comes in pieces (about 30 × 90cm or 1' × 3') and it is, once again, well worth getting a really good quality from an established supplier. There are many rogues around who will cheerfully flog you a lorry-load of ragged, weed-infested turf for what seems at the time to be a bargain price, but will prove to be a poor investment.

It is possible that you may have some surplus turf from another area of the garden, perhaps doomed to disappear under a shed, or be dug over for the vegetable plot. It will make the lifting and relaying easier if you mark out the area to be lifted with pegs and string, into rectangles of the desired size.

Using a piece of timber as a straight-edge, cut with a spade or a half-moon cutter along the sides to about 4 to 5cm (1½" to 2") deep. Then cut across the length at three-foot intervals (or whatever length suits your purpose). Lift the turves by slipping your spade underneath them and moving the spade from side to side to loosen them. When they are free, lift them, roll them up like a Swiss roll, and carry them like this to the area to be turfed, as they are less likely to break when carried in this way. Then lay them out flat in a single layer.

If you find that your turves have all come up in different thicknesses, make a turf tray. Get an off-cut of wood that is about 90cm (3ft) long by 30cm (1ft) wide and nail a batten of the required depth down each side. It is then simple to lay each turf in the tray, (earth side up) and slice off any surplus soil with an old sharp knife. This will make the task of laying the turves much quicker and produce a level lawn.

Lay the turves in rows with staggered joins, like brickwork. Stand or kneel on a plank as you lay each subsequent row, to protect the newly laid turves. It will be easier if you have already marked out the area to be laid with string or timber, and any untidy bits at the sides can be trimmed off with a sharp spade or half-moon cutter, using a straight-edge to keep the line crisp. When you have finished, brush peat between the joins to help the turves to knit up.

Whether you sow or turf, the ground will have to be well prepared beforehand, or you will be wasting your time and money. Having reassured yourself that the drainage is adequate, dig over the ground, removing any large stones and perennial weeds as you go. If the soil is not in good spirits, give a boost by spreading a 2.5–5cm (1"–2") layer of peat, coarse sand and well-rotted manure or garden compost. If you cannot get either of the latter, add a lawn fertiliser or Growmore, following the quantities given on the packet. Rake these into the soil, treading firmly and levelling the surface as you go. Pull a plank or straight-edge of timber across the soil in both directions to make sure that there are no lumps or hollows left, and rake again.

If the weather is dry, give the area a good watering before seeding or turfing. If you are seeding, it helps to mark out the area in square metres with string, as this makes it easier to sow the seed evenly. Ask your supplier to advise you on the most suitable seed for your purposes and site. Late summer and early autumn are usually advised as the best times to sow, but you can sow in spring, once there are signs of growth about, and in early or mid summer, if you can be sure that you will be able to keep the lawn adequately watered. Once you have sown the seed, rake the ground lightly and fix some kind of bird-scaring contraption. Strips cut from plastic shopping bags and knotted round lengths of string make quite good scares, when fluttering lines are stretched out over the lawn.

Turf can be laid at almost any time if the land is not frozen, water-logged or drought-stricken. Again, it should be kept well watered in dry weather, although it can be used right away, the longer you keep people and pets off it until it is well settled and 'knit' together, the happier it will be.

If all this has made you feel quite tired and limp before you start, you could, at a pinch, consider using one of the imitation grass swards I described in Chapter 1. I have to admit to a great deal of prejudice against them, but I also have to admit that I have seen some of them looking very fetching in small urban gardens and on roof gardens. There is some variation between them, so shop around and find one that has some restraint and credibility. They can be brushed, hoovered and hosed-down, all of which takes much less time than the unceasing programme of after-care that the real thing will demand. If you can't afford to buy the stuff, hunt exhibitions and agricultural shows to see if you can buy some from the stands when they close down.

Once your lawn is in place, you will make life easier for yourself if you install some kind of edging which can be mown over. This can be paving stones, a course or two of bricks, tiles, or some kind of curbing, whether it be of stone, concrete or timber. These should all be set below the surface of the lawn so that the mower can pass smoothly over them. If you are laying them to a newly made lawn, allow a little extra depth for settlement. In a wild garden setting, you could use split logs as an edging, and if you have not got enough of your own, you can buy them in rolls at 15, 30 and 45cm (6", 12" and 18") high. If you have any disintegrating panels of interwoven fencing lying about, unweave the strips and use them as a retaining edge, kept in place by wooden pegs—all treated with preservative, of course. Old railway sleepers would make a ruggedly handsome curb, too. Once again, old bricks or lengths of timber, rescued from skips and other glory holes, will be your cheapest solution.

With these major works out of the way, you can turn your attention to the internal features of the garden. Where you have made raised beds, either at one height or in a series of terraced planters, the materials will, once again, need to be in sympathy with the house and nature of the garden. Bricks in a formal setting, or perhaps concrete blocks that have been smoothly rendered and painted over, topped with a neat coping. Stone in areas where it is naturally available, concrete or planed timber in modern settings. Rough timber, railway sleepers, cut logs, sawn lengths of old telegraph poles, peat blocks and what you will in informal country gardens. Those made from bricks, concrete or stone will need to have firm foundations and 'weep holes' for drainage. Remember, when you dig out the trench for the foundations, to keep it covered with plastic sheeting or something similar, to prevent it filling up with water in wet weather before you can finish the job.

Internal divisions and screenings can be 'soft' or 'hard'; that is,

RAISED BEDS

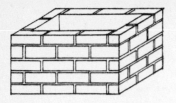

Brick

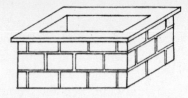

Blocks and coping

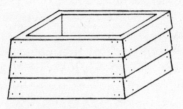

Timber or sleepers

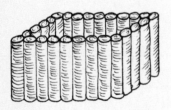

Logs 1

Logs 2

Stacked
hexagons

by planting or by structural means. Planted screens can be formal, e.g. a row of pleached trees, cordon-trained fruit trees, a clipped evergreen hedge; or informal, such as clumps of trees and shrubs, a proportion of which will probably be evergreen. 'Hard' divisions will be similar to those used in the boundaries, i.e. walls, fences, railings and trellises, and once again should be similar in feel to the period and style of the garden. While it is easy enough for an amateur to make low walls of single thickness up to about one metre, anything higher than this calls for expert help or, if you are really dedicated, taking a course in bricklaying—these are some-times available, like many other skills, at local adult education institutes and similar places.

If you do go for internal brick walls, using a honeycomb pattern will certainly be a money-saver. There are pierced-concrete screen-ing blocks available, but once again they look completely wrong in most older types of property or in rural settings. I think that they are only usable in a very modern, urban garden, and then only in their simplest form, in conjunction with a very bold planting of handsome, probably evergreen plants that have an architectural feel, e.g. Fatsias, Palms, Yuccas, Cordylines, Bamboos, etc. There are some openwork terracotta units available which are more attractive, but they are not particularly cheap. Of course, as in any other garden project, if you do the work yourself, the savings can be offset against the price of the materials, but this is only effective if you work within your capabilities. Wobbly walls and undulating terraces are not sensible economies; and they are dangerous to boot.

There are various forms of iron railings and screenings, and the local scrap-metal yards and Architectural Salvage firms are the places to look, while a local blacksmith might run you up some-thing very simple at a not too exorbitant price. These will only make an effective year-round screen if used in conjunction with evergreen planting. A deciduous tree and a climbing rose will look charming in front of the screen all summer, but when winter comes, it will all have a bleak and scrawny air, while any horrors that you have hoped to conceal, such as the garage or the dustbins, will be revealed in all their shame.

Disguising the dustbins is an art in itself and could rate a whole chapter. The old corrugated-metal bins had a certain rugged charm, but their plastic successors are not so appealing. If you have absolutely no space to construct a hide, paint them the same colour as the wall against which they stand. You could spend a happy afternoon painting them in realistic brickwork, perhaps; a piece of trellis could be given a pair of supports and stood in front of them, and if there is room, a potted plant placed in front of this. It will be essential to remove both of these before the dustmen call, or they will be hurled aside contemptuously. Where there is more room, all sorts of little houses can be built for them: from brick, blocks, slates, concrete slabs, trellis, etc. Plants can be trained to grow over them, containers built on top of or placed artfully before them. They can even be given their own doors and, with a suitable, one-way trap, could double up as a place to put the milk until you get home, and/or receive packets too large for your letter-flap. However, it is essential to keep the original function in mind, and easy access to the bins, and their speedy removal when necessary, are of paramount importance.

For an oriental theme, you could nail bamboos to a timber frame, but you would probably have to pre-drill the bamboos before driving nails through them to prevent splitting. Alternatively, you could lash them with twine, to the frame, or buy one of the rolls of split bamboo or cane that are on the market. These would look best with clumps of bamboo planted in front of them, and in conjunction with gravel, pebbles, boulders, etc. They are particularly good for small urban gardens and for balconies or roof gardens.

All of these screens can be used to define areas of the garden, to increase privacy and shelter from the elements for people and plants, and to screen out utility areas and neighbouring eyesores. They can be permanent or temporary, in which case they may well be taken with you if you move (but you must point this out to prospective purchasers). I know of one garden where the owner has used a row of metal hoops, (like outsize croquet hoops) made by the local blacksmith as a garden divider. They are smothered with climbing roses and evergreen climbers, a path wanders through the central hoop and shrubs cluster lovingly round and between the others.

Behind the screening may lie the secret gardens, the children's hideaways or, more prosaically, the various utility areas. A play area can be set up very economically—very small children will be happy with just a sandpit and a paddling pool. For safety reasons, the latter should be a cheap, plastic, ready-made pool which can be emptied at the end of each session to prevent any accidents. All you will have to do is provide a smooth, level surface for it, to reduce the risk of accidents. Grass or sand would do the trick. The sandpit can be made from any materials that you have to hand or can forage for. It is best sunk whole or partially into the ground, with a retaining wall and some form of coping to provide a seat and a surface for mud-pies. The side walls can be made of bricks, blocks, slabs or timber, which should be planed to prevent painful splinters, and treated with preservative. All these materials are easy to find. The flat coping can be made from the same range of materials, and the wider the coping, the better. The larger the sandpit, the more scope there will be for its continued use as the children grow older. Even twelve or thirteen-year-olds have been known to use the sandpit for elaborate layouts of racetracks and battlefields.

Excavate the pit, removing the topsoil and saving it to use elsewhere, as usual. Make the pit about 45cm (18") deep and construct the side walls. If the pit is going to have hard use from older children, it will be worth giving the side walls a good foundation. When the walls are made, place a 5cm (2") layer of fine hardcore or gravel on the bottom of the pit and cover this with a 2.5cm (1") layer of builder's sand. On this lay a base of concrete slabs (broken ones would be fine), leaving 2cm (¾") gaps between them, for drainage. Fill the pit with silver sand or fine, washed builder's sand. The ordinary yellow builder's sand is fine from the

children's point of view but, as I have warned you, it stains their clothes yellow. To keep the sand free from fallen leaves and cats, construct a simple frame of battens to fit over it and nail wire or plastic mesh over the frame. This is quicker, easier, cheaper and better than a solid lid, as the sand will stay sweeter if it is exposed to the elements.

If you have the space and enough materials left over, build a small 'table' at about 45–50cm (18"–20") high, to take a shallow tray of water, for water-play and sailing small plastic or paper boats on. About 10cm (4") of water would be enough and, at that height, should be safe, too. The tray can be made of bricks or timber with a plastic lining. Alternatively, you may find a ready-made tray in your wanderings, some kind of shallow metal or plastic container. I have one that was used to carry loaves round a bakery.

It is quite easy to make simple play equipment for slightly older children out of salvaged materials. A section of log and a planed plank will make a basic see-saw, while a series of logs, sunk into the ground at varying heights, make good stepping stones, and others, topped with planks, would provide an exciting catwalk. If you have a suitable tree, it is easy enough to make swings and trapezes from ropes and bits of wood, while old car tyres, hanging from a branch or beam, are another good bet, and are less likely to cause painful knocks and bruises. If you have the space and a little more skill, you can devise a really ambitious adventure trail from old timbers, with catwalks, monkey-runs, forts, water, ropes and climbing nets, etc.

Quite small children will cherish a 'house' of their own. This can be a wig-wam, made from bamboo-sticks or old broom handles, and they will enjoy it even more if they are allowed to paint their own designs on whatever remnants of material you use to cover the sticks. Primitive ridge-tents or huts, on the lines of Eeyore's, are simple enough to make. Even simpler is an old clothes-horse, with battens nailed across each end to keep it opened out into a V shape, and an old blanket or piece of sacking thrown over it. More permanently, a splendid Wendy-house or shop can be made from foraged bricks, blocks and timber, decorated with all sorts of left-over odds and ends of paint. A remnant of roofing felt or some tough plastic sheeting of the sort that is often wrapped, so impenetrably, round furniture or kitchen units when they are delivered, can be tacked over the roof to keep it water-tight. If you have any old slates or roof tiles lying about, these would give it a very authentic-looking roof.

For older children, a tree-house is probably the most des. res. of all and, with a little help, they will enjoy making it themselves. Give it some kind of roof and they will use it in all weathers, which should give you a much-needed respite, and lead to great savings in alcohol and tranquillisers. The timber used must be sound, of course, and the basic structure strong. The children will prefer a rope or home-made rope-ladder that they can pull up after them, to any fixed ladder. If you do want a fixed ladder, they are made easily enough from bits of wood or the sound sections of old household steps and ladders, fixed in a series of flights from branch to branch. If you have no suitable tree, make them some kind of 'hide' from a planting of evergreens in the most secluded corner of the garden. In my small London garden, four grandchildren have staked claim to a dark corner behind an Arbutus and a couple of Aucubas. The fact that the compost heap is rotting feistily beside them seems to add to the attractions of the spot.

Where space allows, give each of the children their own garden; it may be the start of a lifetime's passion. At worst, it should provide them with some nourishing salad greens, in the form of chickweed and dandelion leaves. I can remember my own first garden very well. A large stone had been placed across the corner of two hawthorn hedges by the kitchen garden. The resulting triangular space had been filled with soil and this primitive raised bed was mine, they told me. Unfortunately, no one thought to tell the cats, who regarded it as a choice *chaise-longue* for their languorous use, and not one of the seeds that I planted so tenderly ever made it to the light. This nearly brought my gardening career to an early stop, but my father came to the rescue and made a special bed for me in a sunny corner of the kitchen garden; well, as sunny a corner as Lancashire could provide. It was four feet square and the earth was retained by six-inch planks, kept in place by wooden pegs or small logs. He added a cinder path round the bed, to deter the slugs, and gave me a starter pack of seeds: Nasturtiums, Love-in-a-Mist, Cornflowers and Larkspurs, all thoroughly satisfactory for a beginner. I progressed to Radishes, Lettuces and more ambitious plantings.

Early successes are important for children; two many failures will probably put them off for life. Start them off with a small patch in a pleasant part of the garden that has reasonable soil, not just any old dingy patch or infertile corner. If there is no room for even these small patches, give them a tub, a sink or even a window-box of their own. Make sure that these containers have a 5cm (2″) layer of drainage material, such as broken crocks, stones or gravel. Fill up with a decent John Innes compost—No.2 or 3—to which you have added a little extra peat and coarse grit. This should give whatever they plant or sow some real chance of success. Older children would also love a raised water-garden, and a discarded butler's or Belfast sink would be ideal. Give it one of the smallest Water-lilies, some submerged oxygenators and one or two floating plants. Leave these to settle down for a week or two before adding some goldfish.

Wherever possible, provide a flat, stable surface for children where they can tricycle, pedal, hop-scotch, roller-skate and skateboard. This is where you *could* use the cheapest concrete slabs, or poured concrete. You may not have room for a tennis court but if you can provide some wall space where they can bang a ball about, it will be a good outlet for their frustration when they are finding life tough (you could try it yourself, too). If there is a window or two on the wall, make a protective cover of battens and chicken-wire or off-cuts of timber, and make some simple retaining gadget of battens and catches so that it is a matter of seconds to slip it on and off. A basket-ball goal-net fixed to the wall would be another good gadget. Any or all of these schemes could buy you a little peace and quiet for a very modest outlay.

St Phocas! I nearly forgot the focal-points . . . and these are the very things which will make sense of your plans and give the garden its balance and style. You will (I hope) have decided on their positions at the planning and laying-out stages, but how to achieve them if antique Corinthian columns are beyond your budget? A superb view would solve at least some of your problems, needing only to be framed by some well-planned planting or revealed by some judicious thinning of existing plants. If the view is hidden by a high wall or hedge, you might be able to cut out a round or lancet shaped 'window' to reveal it. Alternatively, an archway could be cut through and an iron gate, found perhaps at a scrapyard, could be fitted to it, which would still allow the eyes to be drawn through to the prospect beyond.

If you have no such luck, and no existing feature is available to form the basis of your plan, you will have to devise one or more for yourself. Water could be one answer, whether in the shape of a formal lily-pool, a wall-fountain or an informal pond in a wild garden. Pots, ornamental features and garden furniture are all possible choices. Plinths, columns and obelisks can all be made quite easily from bricks or timber and so can simple garden seats. A gazebo or an arbour can also be made from trellis and bits and pieces of wood. When smothered in climbers, any imperfections in their construction will be hidden. Against a wall, you could make a fancy bit of trellis-work, a dashing mural or a mirror-backed arch. Plants that are interesting in form or colour can be planted either singly or in groups as a living feature, and even something as simple as a good plant in an ordinary flowerpot, set perhaps on a raised circle of bricks in a gravelled area, could be a charming and economical solution. If you should happen to be handy with a welding iron, you could make some very striking *objets* from scrap-iron, which would also provide a handy perch for any passing pigeon. Talking of pigeons, it would not be difficult to make a dovecote from bits of wood and oddments of paint, and this could look very fetching in a cottage garden, especially if you installed some genuine fantails. No plastic imitations, please. Finally, if you have the patience, consider the sheer pleasure of a bit of topiary. When completed, it would be both talking *and* focal point. St Phocas would be proud of you (he is, as of course you know, the patron saint of gardeners).

There are several excellent books which describe in detail the necessary techniques to carry out all the projects suggested in this chapter. A list of some of them will be found at the end of the book.

5 MORE SPLASH THAN CASH

Water gardening

Of all the features that a garden can boast, water is probably the most versatile and the most fascinating . . . the reflective tranquillity of still water draws us to it with an almost mystical pull, while the froth and sparkle of moving water entrances and imbues us with some of its energy. Those few fortunates who have natural water on their land are indeed blessed. They can spend delightful hours just contemplating the stuff, speculating idly on future improvements and refinements—a bridge here, a small dam there, a bold planting of Gunnera strategically placed. Yet others of us will have water, not actually on our land but marching with it or as a distant and alluring prospect. Oh happy few, pleasure without responsibility . . .

Some will inherit artificial pools and water-courses installed by the previous owners; these may or may not be blessings. No one could be anything but grateful to have all the hard work of excavation and construction done for them, if the pool is well-sited and pleasing, but more often it sits, an unsightly pimple, on the highest and unlikeliest spot in the garden, lined in virulent blue plastic, encrusted with cement rocks and surmounted by fishing gnomes or an unpleasant youth relieving himself at its edge. It is rare indeed to inherit a well-designed pool, still sound and water-tight, that has been constructed and placed in such a way that it sits happily and harmoniously with house and garden.

Sometimes, however, these existing horrors can be improved. If the pool is in the right place but is leaking or ugly, it can be repaired and given a face-lift. Most manufacturers of liner pools supply repair kits, and water garden centres should be able to advise you about these. If the liners are beyond repair, it will not be too expensive to replace them. If you do not want to remove the existing coping, cut away the old liner, fit the new one in its place, and stick it to the walls with a suitable adhesive, then run a sealing compound round the join. This is only possible if the liner is placed over a solid support, and it is not as satisfactory a method as running the overlap under the coping.

If the leaking liner is fitted over sand or earth, you will have to remove the coping and fit a new liner; it is not really satisfactory to fit one flexible liner over another, as there will be a double set of folds and creases. Make sure that the base and wall of the pool are smooth and free from sharp stones, etc., before fitting the new liner. To make doubly sure, add a layer of damp sand or newspaper at the bottom and up the sides. If the sides are vertical, you could lay another layer of plastic on them under the new liner as protection. Dustbin liners would do, and the tough plastic sheeting which can often be found on skips would be admirable.

Having smoothed the surface in this way, fit the new liner in the manner described by the manufacturers. It is very important to make sure that the liner is in complete contact with the base and side of the pool, as weaknesses will be caused if it pulls away from the side before filling. For this reason, fill slowly, before fitting the coping, so that the water can pull the liner down and press it against the sides of the pool by its own weight. It is absolutely vital to make sure that the sides of the pool are level before fitting the liner. If this is not done, the water will appear to tilt and will drive you mad quite quickly, if you are not already mad (and most gardeners are). Place a spirit-level on a plank across the pool and move this plank all round the pool, checking and levelling firmly as you go.

If the pool is sound, but is a startling blue or an anaemic beige, paint it over with a non-toxic, black waterproof paint. This is not possible with flexible liner pools, but you could revamp these with cheap black liners or even with black polythene sheeting. Alternatively, if you plant the pool thickly enough, not much of the liner below the waterline will be visible; you will just have to disguise the bit between the surface of the water and the coping. Overlapping the coping by about 5cm (2″) over the pool will help to do this. If the pool is straight-sided, you could place lengths of timber just below the coping, or, if there is a ledge, a course or two of bricks could be placed on this. If the pool has a shallow, sloping edge, you could lay shingle or pebbles upon it, and then plant thickly with marginals to overhang the edge, to complete the disguise.

If the leaking pool is concrete, the best solution would be to fit it with a liner. Fill the cracks so that there are no sharp edges to damage the liner. Remove all loose materials and place a 2.5cm (1″) layer of sand at the bottom of the pool as an added precaution, then fit the new liner (this could be performed or flexible) and replace the coping. It is possible to repair concrete pools but it is a tricky job and not always successful. The cracks must be enlarged sufficiently to take a suitable filler (your builder's merchant will advise you), all loose material must be removed and the pool screened over and then coated with a sealing compound.

For any of these methods, you will have to empty the pool, either in whole or in part. If there is no outlet, and no fall away from the pond, you will have to bale it out, a dirty and smelly job. The last couple of inches will have to be mopped up with old towels. If there is a fall away from the pool, you can syphon out the water with a length of hose-pipe. The way to do this is to fill the hose from a tap, sealing both ends with your thumbs, corks, what you will. Then place one end of the hose at the bottom of the pool, holding it in place with a stone or a brick (this, of course, is easier if you have not used your thumbs). It is wise to protect this end of the hose with some fine gauze; a leg cut from a pair of tights will do very well, held in place with a couple of elastic bands. This will ensure that the hose is not blocked with dead leaves, gunge and any wildlife you have been unable to scoop out and remove to safety. Place the other end of the hose as far down the slope away from the pool as possible, preferably into a ditch or drain-trap. If you are doing this single-handed, remove the cork from the pool-end of the hose and run like hell to the other end to remove that cork, too. With luck, the water will then syphon out and away, but do make sure that it is disposed of within your own boundaries; your neighbours will not be amused if they are engulfed and their treasured plants swept away. It may take you a couple of tries to get the syphon working, and you will probably have to scrape unspeakable nasties away from the nylon sock from time to time. The whole thing is much easier with two people and it is always nice to have someone to swear at when things go wrong. You will still have to mop up the bottom of the pond and, if it is to be repainted, give the whole thing a good scrub with detergent and water, then rub down with wet and dry paper to give the paint a key.

Once the pool is sound, watertight and discreet, you can turn your attention to its surroundings. Remove the cement rocks and the manikins. Relocate these (as our American cousins would have it) in the children's garden, donate them to Oxfam, reduce them to hardcore or make a midnight trip to the garden of your enemy and cement them firmly in the middle of his lawn.

If the pool is an irregular one, replace these fancies with turf, gravel, pebbles, small boulders, hunks of local stone (if there is one) and then plant boldly round and between these in an imaginative fashion. No itsy-bitsy Conifers or scarlet Salvias, please.

For a formal pool, make a firm (and when I say firm I do mean firm), handsome coping of whatever materials you can find or purchase for a small sum: slabs, bricks, tiles, railway sleepers, deckings, etc. Remember that, inevitably, the coping will be stood or sat upon. Surround it with level grass, paving, gravel or whatever.

That leaves the rest of us: with no water in the garden, but lusting after it like parched travellers. Even the smallest plot or balcony can provide space for some kind of water; there are plants, including Water-lilies, that will grow in a few inches of water. A tub, a sink, pot or bowl, even a window-box, all could be pressed into service. (See Chapter 8.) Apart from money, there is only one thing that should restrain your enthusiasm or ingenuity: the presence of children or the handicapped. For the latter, some form of raised pool or wall-fountain would solve the problem of them tripping over and into low or surface-level pools, yet they would still be able to enjoy most of the pleasures of water gardening. The blind especially would appreciate the sound of moving water and the scent of Water-lilies.

Children, however, will be quite capable of climbing up and into a raised pool, and even into a tall water-butt. They will be drawn, irresistibly, to such a challenge, in fact they *have* been known to drown in a few inches of water. I believe that small children exhale automatically when they hit the water, which leaves them with no natural buoyancy. If your garden is used by small children, whether your own or visitors', you will have to work out some method of making any existing water features safe for them. For larger ponds and streams, some kind of fence must be erected to keep the children away from the water. You could make these fences yourself, from skip-timber, hurdles or from wire (or plastic) netting, nailed to posts. For a smaller pond, there are several solutions. One is to nail mesh to a wooden batten frame which can be placed over the pool. This is not particularly beautiful but at least the life of the pond can carry on undisturbed. Rather more attractive would be a strong wooden trellis, and another possibility is a panel of cast or wrought iron, or a section of railings rescued from the scrapyard. Only today I saw a beautiful iron grating cover —about 180 × 120cm (6ft × 4ft)—being trundled up the street by the local totter; this would have done splendidly as a pool cover. Fit any of these and the Water-lilies will, at a pinch, flower beneath them, taller plants will grow up through them and the fish won't give a damn, but will carry on about their business in their usual inscrutable way. The protection can stay there until the children have grown to the age of discretion.

Yet another solution is to empty the pond and use it as a sandpit for a few years. Alternatively, the pool can be filled with gravel or cobbles up to or just below the surface (making sure there are no sharp edges to damage the pool—if in doubt put a protective layer of plastic down first), and container-grown plants can be placed amongst the stones. If there is a submersible pump in the pool, it can be given a protective cage, so that it may carry on pumping: a jet of water can spout up from the pool or burble charmingly through and over the stones. Again, all this can be dismantled when the children are older, unless you have become so fond of the effect that you decide to leave it as it is.

In the unlikely event that you might find an old millstone or grindstone lying about, this could be placed across the pool, supported on bricks if necessary, with the pump underneath, to send water bubbling up through the centre hole. Any leftover bits of pool can be filled up with cobbles, as before. If you like this idea but haven't stumbled over any unwanted millstones in the shopping precincts recently, you could make something on the same lines from concrete, poured into a circular shuttering which you have made from skip timber. Smear the inside of the shuttering with soft soap or Vaseline so that it doesn't stick to the concrete. The marks of the shuttering will give an interesting texture to the 'stones'. If the first one turns out a treat, you might be inspired to make various others in different heights and widths, so that your pool would be part fountain, part abstract sculpture.

Those of us less encumbered can let rip within the limits of our budget and our space. From a shallow mirror-pool, reflecting one Hosta and an antique urn, to an ambitious scheme that fills your entire plot, the choice is yours. For the larger, more grandiose schemes, some expense will be inevitable. Even if you don't cost in your own labour and that of anyone you can press-gang in to help, the materials alone will soon add up to quite a sum, unless all of them can be scavenged. You could, of course, stagger these costs by spreading the work over some months or even years. If you are justifying the expense on the grounds that it all adds to the value of

your property, pause a while. Will the next owners *want* a trout or watercress farm, a section of the Grand Union canal, or even waterfalls cascading over limestone outcrops, to take up three quarters of the space available?

If you are gardening on clay, you could, I suppose, try to construct a pool by the old way known as puddling; the basic material being free, you would only have your spare time to spend. The dew ponds were made in this way, but it is, I think, only practicable for a smallish pool. A shallow basin-shaped hole is excavated (to about 60cm (2ft) at its deepest part) which should have sloping sides and a deeper depression in the middle. A thick layer of straw is spread over the surface and a layer of soot placed over this to discourage worms from burrowing through the clay. Then a final coat, of clay, which should be at least 15cm (6") thick, is spread over the pool, kneaded into the straw, puddled down and smoothed over. In theory, the dew will condense on the cold clay walls and trickle down to fill up the pool. Me, I would cheat and use tap water, hoping that the dew might keep it topped up.

If the puddled pool works, you will be awash with pride and perhaps dew; if not, you could turn it into a bog garden, a sandpit or still have your pool by draping black polythene over the hole and decorating its margins in the usual way. Whatever happens, you will have had hours of thoroughly satisfactory mud-play which can only have been therapeutic.

If you have neither clay nor enthusiasm enough for such a project, you are left with a choice between building a concrete pool, fitting a rigid or flexible liner pool, making your own fibreglass pool or utilising some container that you have about the place, or can 'rescue', such as a sink, a bath or a tub. Obviously, if you can find such a container, this will be the cheapest pool of all. Further advice about container pools is given in Chapter 8.

Whatever you decide upon, spend some time considering the style of the pool and its position in the garden. Formal or informal, raised, sunken or flush, still water or moving? In general, irregular pools seldom look at home in a small urban setting, nor when they are set in hard surfaces. They are at their best in a situation where a natural pool would be likely to occur: a low spot in an informal part of the garden, with margins of grass, stones, plants and perhaps some logs. Any water that appears to feed these pools should seem to rise naturally as if from a spring, and run down into the pool through a gentle course or spill from ledge to ledge of a waterfall. Miracles of ingenuity have been accomplished, by way of turning the concrete yard of 2 Alma Terrace into the garden of a Japanese temple, complete with yards of raked sand and pebbles, meandering pools of hideous Koi and Higoi carp, clumps of Bamboo and artfully placed stone lanterns; it is, however, the unquenchable ardour of the owners that one admires, rather than the aesthetic effects thus achieved.

On the other hand the formal pool, whatever its size, looks its happiest in an urban garden or in the more formal parts of a country garden; the terrace, perhaps a courtyard, or at least surrounded by a regular coping, while this in turn may be set in paving, mown grass or gravel, etc. Remember that when you are fitting the pool into coping or paving slabs, it may well be easier to fit the size of the pool to that of the slabs, rather than the other way round, as this will avoid the chore of cutting the slabs, which often leads to several wasted stones.

Here there is a case for some good statuary and a fountain of some sort, but make sure that the water from the jet falls within the circumference of the pool, or an amazing amount of water will be swilling about the place. To prevent this, see that the diameter of the pool is not less than twice the height of the jet, more if the area is a windy one.

Most pools should be placed in an open, sunny position, especially if they are to be planted up. Water-lilies need direct sunlight for at least half the day if they are to flower satisfactorily, although *Nymphaea* 'James Brydon' is supposed to be more shade-tolerant than most. Trees should not be planted too near the pond as their falling leaves will clog it and foul the water, poisoning fish and plants as they rot down. Any large expanse of water could cope

PONDS

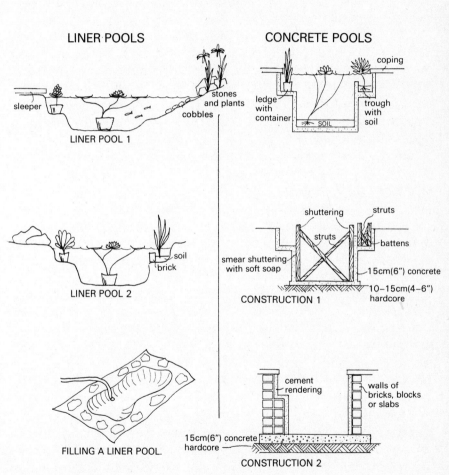

LINER POOLS

CONCRETE POOLS

sleeper

stones and plants

cobbles

LINER POOL 1

coping

ledge with container

SOIL

trough with soil

soil

brick

LINER POOL 2

shuttering

struts

struts

battens

smear shuttering with soft soap

15cm(6") concrete

10–15cm(4–6") hardcore

CONSTRUCTION 1

FILLING A LINER POOL.

cement rendering

walls of bricks, blocks or slabs

15cm(6") concrete
hardcore

CONSTRUCTION 2

with a few trees along the margins, of course, but smaller ponds will be spoilt unless you cover them with mesh in the autumn or scoop them out regularly, both rather boring tasks. Any trees, therefore, should be placed some distance away, preferably to the north or north-east, where they will not take the light but will provide some shelter from the colder winds.

If you have only a shady area available for your pool, it would be better to abandon the thought of Lilies and opt for water instead. By placing a small pump in the pool or installing a wall-fountain, and by surrounding these with easy shade-tolerant plants, such as Bamboo, Fatsias and Hostas, whether in containers or planted directly into the ground, you will be able to enjoy many engaging effects. Having said all this, I have to admit to a sneaking passion for dark, sinister pools, chanced upon in shaded woods, and preferably with the remains of jetties, boat-houses and gazebos rotting on their banks.

As well as requiring sun and shelter from strong winds, the pool should be in an area that is free from the dangers of pollution and serious flooding. In districts of high rainfall, it should be raised above the surface of the surrounding land and given an overflow. At the very least, the coping of a formal pool should be given a slight upwards and inwards tilt so that surface waters do not swill into the pool, especially if there is no overflow device. Overflows are quite easy to install, as are inlet pipes, into pools made of concrete. A length of narrow piping is set in the concrete, just below the coping and above the water line. This leads either to the garden drains, to a ditch or to a soak-away. An outlet for the water can also be constructed on the bottom of the pool, just above the soil level if there is any, by setting a pipe into the concrete, which will lead to the same system as the overflow. This can be fitted with a plug; alternatively a screw-top bottle (such as a cider bottle), with its bottom end cut or broken off, can be set through the wet concrete and into the drain-pipe.

With liner pools, things are a little more tricky. The drainage outlet is not possible, but an inlet pipe and an overflow can be constructed in a makeshift fashion by using a wider gauge of pipe and flattening the pool end to a thin slit, so that this can lie on top of and be stuck to the liner's overlap fitting under the coping or edging. Water will tend to ooze round it to some extent, but more will go down the pipes, with any luck. All overflow pipes should have some sort of grid over them to prevent them becoming blocked or fish being sucked into them. Nylon mesh or perforated metal will do the trick, and the same applies to any outlet pipes.

The availability of water to fill the pool and of a drainage system to remove surplus water from it, should be investigated and if possible installed before work on the pool itself begins. If there is natural water about, it might be possible to channel it to feed the pool and perhaps to make a series of water-courses before it returns to its natural path. Surplus rainwater from roofs and gullies could be led by pipes to some kind of 'reservoir' whose overflow could, at least, top up the pool. Even a permanently dripping overflow from a water tank or lavatory cistern could be channelled in this way. Something of the sort is the ideal solution to prevent the water level dropping and the materials used in the pool's construction deteriorating.

With all these decisions as to site, style and design of the pool out of the way, the excavation work can begin. Having marked out the outline of the pool on the ground, begin to dig, remembering to save the topsoil for use elsewhere. Remember, too, to make sure that the edges of the pool are absolutely level. If you wish to have fish and anything larger than the miniature Water-lilies in your pool, 45cm (18") is about the minimum depth, while 90cm (3ft) should be enough for almost any artificial pool. Even *N.alba*, which is often found in quite deep water, should oblige at that depth (if, however, you do have a large and deep natural pond, it will probably be even happier).

Whatever depth you decide upon, remember to allow in your calculations for a base of 5cm (2") of sand beneath a liner pool. For a concrete pool, you will need to allow for 10cm (4") of hardcore and a 15cm (6") slab of concrete for the base of the pool. The walls, too, will be about 15cm (6″) thick, whether they be of poured concrete or of screeded bricks. If the pool is to have some kind of coping set flush with the ground, this must also be allowed for. Whenever possible, allow for a planting ledge or trough, 20–25cm (8–10″) wide and deep, to accommodate marginal plants. This can be made during the construction of the pool, or afterwards with bricks, etc. Pre-formed plastic and fibreglass pools are usually provided with these ledges, so that you only have to excavate to accommodate them, whilst when making a pool with a flexible liner, you can make the ledge how and where you wish, even providing a central

mound (to take a plant, a stepping-stone or a statue) in the earth, before moulding the liner round it. Any stepping stones should be set, dead-level and firmly fixed, just above the surface of the water, so that they appear to float *on* the water.

Alternatively, both Lilies and marginals can be planted in containers and raised to the appropriate heights on blocks or bricks. There are several excellent books which give clear, detailed descriptions of various types of pool and easy-to-follow instructions for making or installing them. I have suggested one or two of them in the reading list.

This brings us to pools made from 'found' containers. Here the choice is endless. From baths at one end of the scale to an upturned dustbin lid at the other, almost any container can be adapted for use in water gardening. Those that are to be left above ground are covered in Chapter 8, but they can also be sunk into the ground to look like a normal pool. Once again, they will look better if they are given a coat of black waterproof paint or sealant. If they are not absolutely sound, they could still provide a strong base for some black polythene sheeting. However, like all the other pools mentioned, they should be at least 45cm (18″) deep if you intend to keep fish in them, or grow any but the pigmy Water-lilies. If, on the other hand, you are content to use them as mere mirror pools, just a few inches of water will do. You will have to be prepared to empty them and clean them out regularly, as they will be subject to rapid colonisation by algae, the water becoming green and possibly filled with blanket-weed. Shallow water heats up rapidly and this—as well as exposure to light—favours algal growth. A shaded pool will probably remain clear a little longer. There is, in any case, a certain attraction about green water, especially in small town gardens; it looks cool and mysterious. If these shallow containers are merely sunk into the ground and not fixed in by mortar, they will be easy enough to remove for emptying and cleaning purposes.

There was a handsome mirror-pool on show at Chelsea recently, lined with slate slabs and bordered with granite setts. Unless you live in a slate-mining area, you are unlikely to obtain such slabs cheaply but you might, as I said earlier, find the odd large slab lying around, left over from the roof of the outside privy. If you found one or two of these you could get some of them cut to form the side walls and then use the largest piece for the base. You might make a mock-up of this scheme by pressing old roofing slates into wet cement, or use some black quarry tiles instead. The cement could be coloured black by a special stainer.

Any cement that is used in a pool intended for fish or plants will have to be 'cured' or sealed in some way before use, as lime leaches out of fresh cement and is poisonous to pond life. If you make the pool in the autumn, fill and leave it until the spring before emptying and refilling, it should be safe enough. Few of us, however, are so patient. The pool can be filled, left for a few days and then emptied. This will have to be repeated several times. Frances Perry mentions a method whereby a solution of permanganate of potash, strong enough to turn the pool water to the colour of a good red wine, is left in the pool for several days and then the pool is emptied and filled with clean water. There are also various sealers now available at water garden centres. All this will apply equally to any cement you introduce into the pool after construction, for example concrete blocks to hold or anchor plants, and to the cement that holds the coping in place, even if it is above the water line; with heavy rainfall, or if the pool is accidentally overfilled when topping-up, it could still come into contact with the water.

Some metals are toxic to plant life, so it would be as well to paint metal containers on the inside with a black waterproof paint. A dustbin lid, so painted, and sunk to its rim in the earth, could be filled with water and have its margins hidden by turf, pebbles and plants. This would fit into the smallest corner, would give great pleasure to children, and the birds would enjoy it, too. These days, many dustbin lids are made of black rubber or plastic, in which case you would not need to paint them, so it would be even cheaper. They often outlast their bins and, if you cannot find one, ask your friendly refuse collectors if they can lay their hands on one for you.

If you ask them a week or two before Christmas, you are quite likely to have your request granted. Even simpler, just excavate a shallow saucer-shape and line it with black plastic and edge it as usual.

For the deeper pools, use baths, sinks, water tanks and cisterns, plasterer's mixing trays, tin trunks, ammunition boxes, all sorts of metal, ceramic and plastic utensils and containers. Anything, in fact, which is watertight or can be made so by paint, liners or sealants, and has a minimum depth of 45cm (18″), with a minimum surface area of about 0.36 square metres (4 square feet); for example, a pool 60 × 60cm (2′ × 2′) will support a small Lily, some oxygenators and a couple of fish. The usual calculation for the number of fish a small pond can sustain is one fish to each 0.28 square metres (3 square feet) of surface area. Overcrowding can lead to disease.

The larger sized containers can also be used as water-butts. Connected up to the downpipes from the guttering, they will be a useful back-up system for the garden; the water can be used to keep the pools full without the sudden lowering of the water

DUSTBIN LID POOL

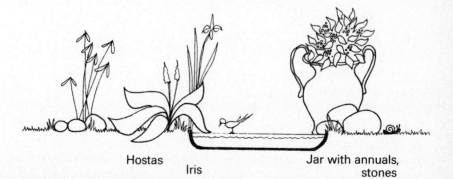

Hostas

Iris

Jar with annuals, stones

temperature which comes from filling them from a tap (this affects the balance of the pool life), for watering plants that are intolerant of lime and for bringing on new water-plants until they are ready to go into the larger pool. A lot of plants are happier when sprinkled with this warmer water, rather than having to face the short sharp shock of tap-water.

Old casks and barrels make good sunken pools; on a sloping site you could place a series of them, one beneath the other, down the slope, sunk to their rims and, once again, framed by logs, pebbles and plants. The top one can be filled up from time to time and allowed to overflow into those below, if there is no natural flow to do this for you. The larger and deeper the cask the better. They must be cleaned out thoroughly and, if necessary, sealed.

The really masochistic could consider making their own fibre-glass pool. If you have some experience of working with the stuff it would help; boating enthusiasts and DIY car-repairers come to mind. It is beastly to work with, so you would need all the protective clothing you can get on, including rubber gloves and a face mask (from builder's merchants). Use very old clothes that you can throw away afterwards. Dig out the shape required and line it with damp newspaper. Cut out lengths of the fibreglass and then mix up the resin and the catalyst, but not all at once as it goes off quickly. You can smear the lining paper with this and then the lengths of fibreglass. Press these into position round the pool in an even layer, overlapping them and smoothing and pressing them against the sides of the excavation as you go. When the whole pool is covered in these overlapping layers, apply a final coat of the resin/catalyst mix and smooth it off. You can obtain a black dye which is added at the resin-mixing stage, or paint the pool after-wards.

If you are going for a fashionably conservationist wildlife pool, make it by any of the foregoing methods, preferably with an irregular shape, in the wildest part of the garden or in a field if you have one. Make it with the usual stepped ledges or troughs for marginal plants and give one side a shallow sloping bank, in which

birds can frisk and up which hedgehogs and other feckless creatures can, one hopes, regain the land. This pool should, ideally, be
allowed to fill with rainwater and have a bucket or two of old pond
water added to it to speed things up a bit. Try to keep to native
water plants, be they Lilies, submerged, floating or marginal
plants. Native fish are the thing here and as many frogs, newts and
other locals as you can persuade to linger. You can wait for them to
arrive or ask around from other pond owners who will be only too
grateful to thin things out a bit. It is illegal to dig up wild plants but
you can grow some of them from seed. Give your pool a variety of
margins: coarse sand, shingle, stones, logs, turf and plants, with
areas of sun and shade, to give the widest range of habitat for the
inhabitants. A few native shrubs and, beyond them, some trees,
will complete the amenities of this prestigious development.

Unless you have a source of natural water to hand, all the other
pools will have to be filled from tap-water. Let this stand for several
days to allow the chlorine to evaporate and the water to warm up a
bit. Then add the oxygenators, the floating aquatics and the
marginal plants. Finally add the Water-lilies. These should be
raised up on some kind of support, such as old bricks or an
upturned plastic flower pot, so that the crowns are just below the
surface. They can be lowered gradually as they grow until they are
large enough to be placed on the bottom. At all stages their leaves
should be just floating on the water, not below. Remember to
weather any bricks or concrete blocks if you use these to support
the Lilies.

Most plants these days are grown in containers, which makes it
easy to lift them and repot every three years. However, they will
grow very well in about 15cm (6") of good heavy loam, preferably
the top-spit, stacked in the autumn, sandwiched with cow-manure
and allowed to rot down for six months at least. Urban dwellers
may find this hard to come by. In this case, use any good bits of
top-spit loam, shorn of its grass and mixed with a handful of
sterilised bonemeal to each bucketful of loam. If you have no spare
turves, friends in the country could oblige. You can make your own

slow-release booster by forming balls of bonemeal and clay, and pushing these down by the roots of the plants, whether container-grown or free growing. Top the loam (and the surface of containers) with 2.5cm (1″) of pea-shingle to keep the soil in place and frustrate the rootling fish.

As for the plants, many water garden centres will sell you a mixed bunch of oxygenators, all or some of which will thrive in your pool. In very small pools, you could try Vallisneria, suggested for container pools in Chapter 8, since the normal oxygenators can spread very rapidly. Your choice of Water-lilies will depend on the size of your pool, and its depth. A few have already been mentioned in this chapter, and some for container-sized pools are given in Chapter 8. The books listed at the end of this book describe what is available. If your pool has room for only one or two marginals or aquatics, you could still have something in flower for most of the summer, by keeping a reserve selection of container-grown plants in a tank, somewhere out of sight, and whipping these in and out of your pool as they come into and out of flower.

Planting is best done in the growing season—late spring, early summer—and the plants should be allowed to start into active growth for a week or two before adding any fish. Common goldfish, comets and golden orfe are the ones I would go for. If they arrive in a plastic bag, open and place this on the surface of the pool for about 20 minutes so that the fish has time to acclimatise to the temperature of the pool. On a hot day provide some shade during this period. Then tip the fish gently into the pool. Your children may return with some unfortunate fish from the local fair, or various friends and neighbours may have surplus fish as well as plants to dispose of. Otherwise, local pet shops and water garden centres are the places to look. It would be as well to have some water-snails in addition to the fish, to help the balance of life in the pond. You want the Great Ramshorn Snail for this (*Planorbus corneus*), not the pointed Great Pond Snail (*Limnea stagnalis*) which will devour your Water-lilies. If it does arrive and decide that your pool is home-sweet-home, float a lettuce or a cabbage leaf on the surface of the water overnight, and in the morning pick off the beastly things from the underside. Repeat this at intervals to keep the pond free.

It will take some time for the pool to settle down and, initially, it will almost certainly turn pea-green with algae. Be patient, and eventually the water will usually become clear. Do not be tempted to empty the pool and start again, or you will be back to square one and have to go through all the waiting time once more before things improve. If the pool needs topping up during this time, try to use rainwater, so as not to disturb the balancing process. Very rarely, things will not clear up and you will have to ask for professional advice from the water garden centre, or a 'pond doctor'. Meanwhile you can remove surface scum from small pools by dragging a newspaper across the surface, and pull out blanket-weed by hand or with a stick. From time to time your water plants may need thinning and dividing; then you can do a little canny trading with other gardeners, a good way to improve the variety of plants in your pool.

When everything in the pool has settled down and is being sensible, as my old headmistress would have put it, you can sit back and enjoy it, reclining like the pensive Selima, with merely the odd scattering of fish food to see to, and the removal of over-enthusiastic inhabitants or unwelcome visitors, who have just 'dropped in', as it were. However, in the winter, you will have to take some steps to keep the fish healthy during periods of freezing weather (which can also damage the pool itself). A child's rubber ball, or several of them, floating on the surface, will help, as will small pieces of wood. When thick ice does form, do not break it up as fish are very sensitive to vibrations and could be killed. Place a saucepan of boiling water to stand on the ice until it has made a hole right through. You will have to repeat this every day to allow toxic gases to escape. This will be especially necessary if there are rotting leaves in the pool.

If the fish feel really at home, they may breed. Unfortunately, the parent fish are perfectly happy to devour their young and, when possible, should be removed to another pool or container for a few weeks after spawning, to give the fry a chance to grow. However, if you are making your own pool, you can provide a trough at the side with a sufficiently high side to make sure that only the fry, not the parent fish, can swim into it. This trough will also need some shade and shelter for the fry, provided by aquatic plants, stones and perhaps an artificial fish shelter of the sort sold for aquariums. A bit of old slate could be propped up by some stones or some cured bricks to provide a refuge for battered babies. These can also by installed in the main part of the pool, to give the adult fish a 'hide' before the plant life gives them sufficient cover.

You can provide a form of food for the fry called Infusoria. Place a lettuce leaf in water for a few days and the Infusoria will appear. A banana skin covered with rainwater and enriched with a couple of teaspoons of milk should also provide some. Other delicacies that the fish will appreciate are chopped earthworms (*another* use for the magimix) and water-fleas which I feel you are unlikely to have about your person but which you could probably attract by providing a small container of fishless water, with some loam and bonemeal at the bottom. Once you have them, they will increase and multiply in a way that would embarrass even the Pope.

Fish should never be overfed, and any food left uneaten after about five minutes should be scooped out and removed. Spring and autumn are the most important times to feed; to build them up for, and to help them recover from, the lean winter months. If, on a hot day, you see the fish gulping for air at the surface, this means that they are short of oxygen. Stir the water a bit, run in some more and check that the pool is not overstocked.

Both fish and water plants are sometimes available in bargain collections from garden centres; this can be a cheap way to stock up your pool, and then you can swap some of them with neighbours who have found different collections, when you have enough to spare.

With the pool made and stocked, you can consider its margins and surroundings. With the formal pool, there is very little needed except a solid coping of some kind and possibly a statue, if you happen to have a good one about you. It is quite difficult to buy an acceptable statue without parting with a sizeable sum. This is where friendly art students could come in useful. If you don't know any, contact the sculpture class at the local art school or college of adult education, especially when they have their end-of-term shows.

Even better, attend such a class and make your own sculpture. If you already have a bit of talent, you can make a basic shape of crumpled chicken-wire and build on to this with cement, layer after layer. Anything largish will need a basic armature of metal; rods or angle irons, etc., to support the wire and cement. When you have achieved a satisfactory shape, you can paint it black, to resemble lead, a greenish copper shade, or stain the whole thing down with liquid manure when it will look quite a lot like weathered stone (yes, really, it will).

Another idea to adorn the formal pool is a container of some kind, either empty or planted up. This could be as simple as an ordinary clay plant-pot, filled with geraniums, or whatever you can find or lug home from foreign parts. It really is possible to pick up some very handsome pots, even in the tourist spots, at reasonable prices, and so long as they don't exceed your weight allowance, it will be worth the effort of getting them back. One of my favourite gardens has a large Turkish coffee-pot, of beautifully greened copper, standing by the pool. It was rescued from a closing down café in a country town and, despite its exotic origins, looks very much at home in this Hampshire garden. Some simple urns and pitchers can be used, placed on their side at the edge of the pool, as a gentle fountain, with water pouring from the lip, and returned, by some discreet piping and a submersible pump. Once again, the place to look for these include auctions, jumble sales, junk shops, etc. Even quite unpromising shapes can be used as the basis for your skills. Hideous colours can be painted over, ugly shapes could be used as armatures and built upon, etc., etc.

For the informal pool, there are many choices: plants, stones, boulders, pebbles, logs or various combinations of these, with areas of turf and perhaps a bench, of some rugged sort, so that one can sit and meditate. This last, of course, would be useful, in a slightly more sophisticated shape, by the formal pool. The irregular pool is not the place for statues, except just possibly a particularly strong-shaped abstract, more boulder-like than spiky. An interesting natural boulder or rock could look right, and so could a log or piece of driftwood. Anyone lucky enough to find a large fossil, such as an ammonite, could try it by the pool to see if it looked happy, whilst the morbid might settle for a cattle-skull amongst the Hostas.

Fountains do not belong here and besides, the Water-lilies do not much care for moving water, although if the pool is large enough you could have water gurgling gently into the pool from a stream, natural or man-made, while planting Lilies in a calm patch at the other side.

When recommending plants, there are so many that it is difficult to single out a few, but in general, those that are in nature associated with water margins will look the most convincing. For the borders of large pools, the Gunneras, Rheums and Rodgersias are magnificent. If you have a sufficiently skilful eye to be able to juggle proportions about and break rules, you can even place one of these monsters in a small garden to great effect. They need a moist but not waterlogged soil.

If you do not have such an obliging bit of land you can contrive one, by excavating the area you require to about 30–60cm (12″–24″) deep and lining this with polythene. Quite a cheap quality will do, as it does not have to be water-tight, just moisture retentive, by slowing down the drainage. The excavated soil should be mixed with peat, leaf-mould, well-rotted compost and some bonemeal. Prick drainage holes through the side of the plastic, starting an inch or two above the bottom in some places, a bit higher in others, so that small reserves of water will be retained but not enough to allow the soil to become sour and water-logged. Then return half the enriched soil, and lay a length of hose-pipe along it, either in one line or snaking about on a larger area. The far end of the hose should be blocked off in some fashion and holes pierced at about 15–20cm (6"–8") intervals along the pipe. The business end should be brought to the surface near to the water supply, and be fitted with a hose connector. During dry periods, water can be run through the hose to keep the soil moist, while in winter and periods of serious rainfall, things would look after themselves. Flagging foliage will be a sign that you need to intervene and let the water run through again.

Gunneras are susceptible to frost damage. They can be protected by wrapping their own leaves round their crowns in late autumn, and tying these in place. A further mulch of bracken or peat, etc., can be piled over this for extra comfort. In this cosy wig-wam, they should make it through till spring.

It is not a good idea to moisten these artificial bogs by overflowing the pool, as the introduction of sufficient cold water to achieve this will upset the balance of the pool to a serious extent.

Plants that will enjoy these semi-bog conditions include the Filipendulas, Hostas, Primulas, Mimulus, Lythrums, Astilbes, Aruncus, Hemerocallis, several Iris, and many others, as well as the aforementioned giants. Several of them can be grown from seed, cuttings and divisions, so that you should be able to plant quite reasonably, and do remember to do this in good bold groups, not in irritating dots. Anything mimsy and whimsy is quite wrong here (and everywhere else, for that matter).

The true bog plants and marginals will be happiest in a few inches of water on a ledge or trough near the pool's edges (the more vigorous of them in containers to restrain their enthusiasm). These would include *Calla palustris*, *Caltha palustris*, *Iris pseudacorus*, *I. pseudacorus* 'Variegata' and *Pontederia cordata*. Again, there are many others, described in books mentioned in the reading list.

Beyond these waterside plants come the shrubs and trees. The Willows, of course, in variety, but do not make the common mistake of planting the well-known Weeping Willow anywhere near a small pool. It is one of the most beautiful trees when planted by large areas of water, but will quickly overhang and clog smaller ponds. *Salix purpurea* 'Pendula' is the tree for these smaller pools, while the Kilmarnock Willow, *Salix caprea* 'Pendula', would be in scale by even the merest apology of a mirror pool. Its long branches are a little stiff, perhaps, but it has a charm all of its own, and is hung with 'pussies', bright as moonstones, in the spring.

After this come the Cornus, in variety: *C. alba* and var. 'Elegantissima', *C. stolonifera*, *C. stolonifera* 'Spaethii' and *C. stolonifera* 'Flavirama' (with yellow stems) are among the best. The Bamboos and Grasses are good here, too; I am very fond of Alders, and these can look good in the wilder garden by a medium to large sized pool.

You will have to shop around for all of these to find them at bargain prices, or on special offers; some you will be able to grow from cuttings, divisions and seeds, if you have time and space enough.

All gardeners have their little whims and prejudices. My particular bugbear is a rockery. Oh yes, I know, I know, the plants are fascinating, and anything miniature has a special charm, but unless you have a natural outcrop or can afford tons of rock to be imported and installed in your garden, which can, when skilfully done, look magnificent, especially with water cascading through from ledge to ledge (and even then I am not entirely happy about it), you are better off without them. As often as not, they are a dazzling blaze of eye-aching colour for a week or two in spring, and a weed-infested horror for the rest of the year, with unconvincing nobs and bobs of stone set at unlikely angles on a mount of subsoil left behind by the builders. Even when knowledgeably made and planted, they take hours of hand-weeding to keep in top form, and I have better things to do. As a surround to the water garden, I have yet to see one that I lust after, and I would find other homes for the alpine plants. Just think of the time and money you can save by *not* having a rock garden, whether beside your pool or anywhere else . . .

As for streams, canals and watercourses, they can be made in the same way as the pools; that is, by concrete or rendered bricks and blocks, by pre-formed units, and by liners. You can make your own pre-formed waterfall units, from concrete or fibreglass. Simply make some small basin or saucer shapes in the soil, line with newspaper, and coat with concrete or fibreglass, both of which could be stained at the mixing stage. Give these little basins a slight lip, so that water can fall smoothly from one to another. When you have enough of these shapes for your purpose, fit them into your slope, fiddling around until you get the flow and fall of the water just right, and then bed them down firmly and disguise their edges in the same manner as you used for the pools.

More formal courses can be made in bricks, blocks, etc. If you have made a flight of brick steps, consider the making of another, narrow flight, just alongside, and allowing water to flow down this to a brick pool, to be returned to the top of the slope by a pump . . . once you get the hang of this sort of thing there will be no stopping you.

As for bridges over your streams, these are easily made from a variety of salvaged materials. Over a very narrow stream, a simple flagstone would be perfect. For something a little wider, a few railway sleepers would do, or a simple cross-over of skip timber, made by placing two strong pieces to cross the stream and nailing logs, planks or battens to these. Alternatively, search the scrap-metal yard, etc., for a suitable piece of cast iron, such as a balcony floor or grating cover. Handrails can be made in matching materials when necessary. These can be as simple as one rail or rustic branch, nailed to posts on each bank, or something vaguely oriental, in the same sort of pattern as those suggested in Chapter 4. If you have found a piece of iron for the bridge, you might be able to find an iron handrail or short section of railings to go with it. You can make a mock-up of iron railing by fitting dowels into two lengths of batten (about 5×1.5cm ($2 \times 1\frac{1}{2}''$) or $\times 2$cm ($\frac{3}{4}''$) would do), and painting it all glossy black. The supporting posts could be topped by some kind of wooden finial, such as those used to finish newel-posts or curtain rails; these are found easily enough at timber merchants or DIY shops—one way or another you have hours of fun ahead.

6   LEAF IT OUT

Planting and propagation

Planting is one of the most deeply satisfying of earthly tasks. In ideal conditions it becomes positively sensual. To sink one's fingers into the friable soil (no, not old wrapping paper from fish and chips), settle the plant into its new home, press it kindly and firmly into place and water it in—oh what joy, as the song says. Squelching round in cold, wet clay is not so sensuous (though I dunno, on second thoughts . . .) but to dig in a mass of soil improvers, then watch the plants grow up gracefully and, one hopes, gratefully, is possibly even more rewarding; the feeling of hardships shared and overcome, I suppose.

Although in these days of container-grown plants, planting can be carried out at almost any time of the year, if the ground is not frozen, sodden or drought-stricken, early to mid-autumn is a favourable time for many plants. The soil still has enough warmth to encourage them to settle in and make some root-growth, yet there is less likelihood of prolonged dry periods and scorching. Conifers are traditionally planted in September or April, while the more tender plants, including many of those with silver leaves, are best left until late spring unless you are in a very protected spot. Roses are happiest when planted bare-rooted, at any time between November and March; they usually get away better than container-grown roses, which are more expensive, but handy to fill in gaps or replace losses.

Few of us will take over a garden where the soil is in peak condition: a rich, dark, crumbly and nutritious loam. Before planting begins, and preferably about a month in advance, we should start to improve the soil. To begin with, clear the land of any perennial weeds, roots and all. The latter may need one or two doses of weed-killer if you have large areas to deal with and not all that much time. I like to keep the use of chemicals to a minimum in the garden, and prefer to use organic methods whenever possible, but, like most of us, I suppose, take the easy way out from time to time. Annual weeds can be removed to the compost heap.

As mentioned in Chapter 3, compost is probably the best and certainly the cheapest soil improver of all, equally valuable on soils that are too light as well as those that are too heavy; improving the structure of the soil while increasing its nutrition and moisture retention. Leaf mould is another wonderful soil improver. However, even if you have room for a row of compost-heaps and leaf-bins, it will be some time before the contents are ready for use. Even the best and most efficiently-made compost will take some weeks to rot down in the summer, and some months in the winter, while leaf mould will take a year or two at least. By all means start a heap, but until it has turned itself from a dodgy-looking mess of squashed layers, like a giant's vegetable terrine, into something more like the contents of his tobacco pouch, crumbly and sweet-smelling, you will have to look elsewhere. The smaller you chop your compost and leaves, the quicker they will rot down, so that, as I said in Chapter 3, if you do have a large garden to deal with, it might be worth investing in one of the compost-shredding machines; its cost could soon be recouped by the savings in peat, etc. Certainly, small quantities of kitchen waste can be put through the blender or food-processor, but this is a small-scale solution for small-scale gardeners, or for spot-feeding. I once had a shy-flowering Banksian rose which responded magnificently to a dietary supplement of liquidised banana-skins and old tea-bags. You can, as I mentioned before in connection with bracken, put leaves and compost into a bucket and chop savagely with a pair of shears, which should speed things up a bit, whilst brassica stalks and corn-husks should be chopped up with an axe before being added to the heap; but even with all this vicious treatment, things will take time. Material that has not completely rotted down will deprive the soil of nitrogen rather than add goodness to it, although the structure will still be improved. Economical and organic gardeners could not do better than read Dick Kitto's book, *Composting*, a wonderfully comprehensive guide to the subject; it describes how to construct the bins, how to fill them and how to use the compost, as well as having a chapter on 'green manures'; that is, plants, such as Mustard, Lupins, Clover, Fenugreek, etc., which you sow in the ground, allow to grow until the crop is a few inches high and then dig or rotovate back into the soil. *Organic Gardening* and *Down to Earth Gardening*, by Lawrence D. Hills, are both marvellous 'reads' and veritable mines of information on all aspects of organic (and therefore economical) gardening. If you intend to grow your own produce, his book *Grow your own Fruit and Vegetables* is excellent, too.

Those who have no room for compost-heaps or leaf-bins can still, as I said in Chapter 2, make compost by storing the material in plastic sacks or fertiliser bags. Put leaves in one, garden and kitchen waste in another. Fasten them tightly at the neck and pierce them with a fork to let in some air. You can add an accelerator to the bags, as you do to the heaps, to speed up the process, using fresh manures, a commercial product or what Mr Hills calls Liquid Household Activator (diluted urine to you and me).

If you do have room for some containers, they can be made easily from any salvaged materials, about 90cm (3ft) square; two would be better than one; in fact the more the merrier. Leaf-bins can be made by driving four posts into the ground and nailing wire-netting to them (not larger than 4cm (1½") mesh or the leaves will escape).

If your garden does not supply enough leaves and vegetable matter for your needs, you will have to scrounge around for extra. Chat up the road sweeper or the park-keeper. Mr Hills promises that even Plane tree and Sycamore leaves will rot down in time. Ask your less thrifty neighbours and friends if you can have their leaves and weeds. Pensioners, particularly, would be grateful to have the clearing-up of leaves done for them. You can ask the local hairdresser and barber to save their floor sweepings, as unless you have a large and hirsute family, you are unlikely to be self-sufficient in either hair or nail clippings, both of which can go on the heap. In return for weeding and sweeping the churchyard, you could get plenty of organic material plus the kind thoughts and prayers of the vicar, thus improving your soul along with your soil, an economic double. As well as kitchen waste (but not greasy or animal matter, which could attract vermin) and the garden waste, excluding permanent weeds and diseased material, you can add old newspaper and paper bags, torn up and moistened in small quantities at a time. Do not use colour supplements or magazines, as some of the inks may be toxic. Spent hops, old mushroom compost, seaweed, green bracken and manures in variety, can all be added to your heap. Lawn mowings should be mixed up with other materials, not added in a layer, or they will form a slimy mess.

If you are lucky enough to find a supply of well-rotted manure, it can be added to the ground straight away. Horsy friends, riding stables, racing stables, etc., are often glad to dispose of their surplus, either for free or for very little money. Try to get it from the older heaps, but if that is not possible, you will have to store it under cover for some months, until it is sweet and crumbly. Fresh manure would only scorch your plants, and should not be applied straight away.

For many years I had a cottage by the sea in Hampshire and would send my children out to fetch seaweed. They absolutely hated this, dying with embarrassment every step of the way, and it is still brought up as a grievance at family reunions. The garden, on the other hand, loved the stuff and devoured barrow-loads. I dug bucketfuls into the bottom spit and spread more over the surface, chopping it up a bit and forking it into the topsoil. Never again have I been able to grow Sweet Peas of such size, scent and colour. Sandy soils, in particular, will enjoy the addition of seaweed.

Once you get bitten by the gardening bug, all restraint and

shame will be forgotten; you will importune friends, neighbours, nay, your merest acquaintances and total strangers, for organic material, begging them to bring you back leaves, manure and seaweed from jaunts to the country. Your own car will begin to smell like the breeches of ancient gardeners—a mixture of mould, rot and incontinence. Dawns will find you tip-toeing towards the compost heap, buckets of night-soil in hand; you will eye the plants of your neighbours with more lust than you feel for their bedmates and you will have to fight off the most hideous temptations towards the nipping of cuttings from the gardens of the National Trust and the municipal parks. But I digress; back to the soil.

If you have no time to wait, and no space, for all this teeming life to transform rubbish into treasure, you will have to resort to what you can buy in the way of peat, bark, commercially-composted manures and chemical fertilisers. They do not come cheap, so it is important to use them sparingly and where they can do most good. They can be bought from shops, garden centres and specialist firms. Look through the local papers, gardening magazines and the Yellow Pages for these. Remember that large quantities are nearly always cheaper, so see if you can join up with your neighbours and share an order. This is always worth a try, whether ordering sundries, plants, construction materials or hiring machinery.

Home-made composts and free or cheap manures can, if you have enough of them, be spread generously across the land, but anything for which you have had to fork out your hard-earned cash should be husbanded carefully. First make sure that you are using the right stuff at the right time, in the right place and in the right quantities. Too much can be worse than too little, and misplaced kindness can kill as surely as neglect. Place a suitable amount of peat, compost or fertiliser in each planting hole as you go, rather than dig it into the whole trench. Plants can be fed, sprayed and mulched individually rather than in mass operations, much as you would like to be more liberal. Chopped-up newspaper can be moistened and put at the bottom of planting holes for thirsty plants and be spread as a mulch between others, hidden by a sprinkling of soil to keep it in place. Individual plants have their little whims and ways; it will pay to study them and treat them accordingly, rather than to supply them with luxuries that they may not need. Some plants prefer a poor soil, so it would be foolish to enrich it.

It makes economic sense to grow only those plants that will be happy in your soil and climate rather than waste time, energy and money on changing the soil and persuading some pernickety thing to grow in it. If your soil is moist and boggy, grow those plants that will revel in it, but remember that very few will thrive if the soil is actually waterlogged. Other plants will benefit from a dry, fast-draining position, although they will still need to be watered when young and in periods of prolonged drought. There are plants for shade, whether dry or damp; plants for sun or dappled shade, for slopes and hollows; plants that thrive in an acid soil, others that will enjoy or tolerate lime; whilst the vast majority will settle for something in between. If you absolutely must have a plant that will not thrive in your conditions, grow it in an enclosed bed or container so that its special requirements can be ministered to in small quantities. An alpine garden in a trough, and a Rhodo-dendron in a tub are two examples of this approach.

Wherever you plant, I must stress again that it will be essential first to rid the ground of perennial thugs like ground-elder, couch-grass and bindweed. If you neglect to do this, they will entwine themselves round and through your treasures, which will prob-ably give up the struggle to survive. It will be virtually impossible to eradicate the weeds once they have become so entrenched and entangled; better to put off planting until the ground is clear.

Having cleaned and enriched your soil as best you can, and then made sensible decisions about the types of plant that are likely to succeed without too much fuss, you can begin to plant, consulting your plans as you go. Ideally, all the ground should have been prepared well in advance and allowed to settle, but this may not be possible, so carry on, firming the plants well in, and be prepared to check them from time to time as the soil settles, adding or subtracting the soil around them when necessary. When planting trees and shrubs, the soil should come to the same level on their trunks or stems as it did when they were in their previous site or container. This is usually quite clear from the soil-mark on the bark. If it is not, aim to have about 5cm (2") of soil over the topmost roots.

If you are planting a hedge as a boundary, this will probably be your first task. Here again, thorough preparation of the soil will make all the difference to the health and survival rate of the plants. It makes sense to dig out a trench, about 90cm (3ft) wide and 60 cm (2ft) deep, for large plants. Fork up the subsoil a bit and return half the earth to the bottom of the trench, adding and mixing to it as much compost and rotted manure as you can spare. Failing these, add a little peat and granular fertiliser, such as Growmore, under the roots of each plant as you go. Space the plants out well, up to 90cm (3ft) apart for *leylandii*, and put them in position, giving them a stake or wires if necessary. Then return the remainder of the soil and firm the plants in. Give them a good watering and keep them clear of weeds, and fed and watered for the first few years, until they are well established. Remember that small plants, 90cm (3ft) or thereabouts, will be cheaper (with further reductions for larger orders) and get away better than large plants, as a rule. They will have time to form a good root system before growing high enough to be buffeted by the winds. If you are not sure how to space the plants, consult the catalogues, reference books or a good nurseryman.

Many people will choose an evergreen hedge both for the privacy it will provide and for the handsome backdrop it makes for other plants. For a tall hedge, of about 2m (7ft) upwards, *Cupressocyparis leylandii*, its golden form 'Castlewellan', and *Thuja plicata*, are all good bets and comparatively cheap. For a medium 1–2m (4–7ft) hedge, Yew is the noblest of them all, but no one could call it cheap unless you are prepared to propagate the plants yourself. Holly makes a lusty barrier and is boldly sombre in its green forms, cheerful in the variegated ones. *Chamaecyparis lawsoniana* 'Green

Hedger' is pleasing and *Escallonia* is a beautiful hedge for milder or seaside positions. Cheapest of all the evergreens are the much despised Privets and Loniceras. Privet in particular is a greedy feeder, robbing the soil around it of nutriments. Certainly, when neglected and lanky, they are poor, miserable things, but well grown, fed and clipped (often), they make a neat enough hedge and a solid barrier. Both have golden forms which give a welcome brightness in the long winter months, especially in towns and suburbs, as well as providing useful material for winter flower arrangements. They grow fast, are cheap to buy and grow easily from cuttings. Incidentally, all the privets make splendid small trees and can be trained easily enough as single-stemmed specimens, or planted, three in one hole, to produce an instant multi-branched wonder.

For non-evergreen, but still fairly formal hedges, Beech in its green or purple forms makes a good choice. The dead leaves stay on the branches throughout the winter, which is a love-it or loathe-it effect, so look around you to help you decide. Cheapest of the deciduous hedges are probably *Prunus cerasifera* (cherry plum), *Prunus spinosa* (sloe), Hornbeam and Hawthorn. I am devoted to the latter, bringing as it does memories of a splendid 2.75m (9ft) hedge surrounding one of the gardens of my childhood. For less formal hedges, the choice is wide, from the evergreen Pyracanthas and Berberis to the hardy and long flowering Rugosa Roses. Look around you again, and consult reference books and local nurserymen. For internal hedges and screens, almost anything goes, if it takes your fancy and will not outgrow the available space, except those plants that are so noble in shape that they need to be seen in virtual isolation to look their best; the Magnolias are a good example. Look out for bargains in the press and local garden centres as prices can vary considerably. This applies to all plants, but particularly to hedging, I think.

With the boundaries and perhaps the internal hedges and screens planted, you can turn your attention to those trees or shrubs that are to provide the focal point (or points) of your garden;

those, that is, which will, singly or in groups, attract and distract the eye, according to your plan. These will need the most careful siting of all, and on this much of the success of your garden will depend. Except for a few rare, tender or a very slow-growing varieties, trees are among the most amazing bargains to be found today. For somewhere between ten and twenty-five pounds you can buy a thoroughly satisfactory ornamental tree about 2–2.5m (5–8ft) tall which will, with a little care, be your pride and joy for years to come, and give pleasure to others after you, to boot. Some of these are very fast-growing indeed. The Eucalypts, for instance, can be planted as mere wisps of silvery-blue, 90cm (3ft) high, which in three or four years may be soaring up and bushing out at a rate that can be positively embarrassing if you have put them in the wrong place. In the right place they look splendid and can be cut back to near ground level to supply a succession of juvenile foliage, or pollarded in restricted space. I like them planted in groups of three to form a small grove. *Robinia pseudoacacia* 'Frisia Aurea' is another rampageous grower which, alas, because of the appealing colour of its fresh, green-gold leaves, is often seen in the small front gardens of terraced houses. There, in about four or five years, it will have shot up to the eaves and be taking every vestige of light from the front parlour. Given space to billow out and perhaps planted where the evening sun can shine through its leaves, it is a delight.

Trees should have a good wide hole dug out for them and the soil enriched in the same way as for the hedging plants. Give them a strong stake while they are young and fasten them to this with either a plastic tree-tie or with pieces cut from a pair of old tights. These are quite efficient, if not exactly elegant, having enough 'give' in them to avoid damage to the young bark of the trunk. *All* ties should be checked regularly to make sure they have not become too tight. Again, the soil around them should be mulched and kept free of weeds for some years to give them every chance to establish themselves. All mulches should be applied over moist soil, when the sun has warmed the earth up a little in the spring, or

TREE PLANTING

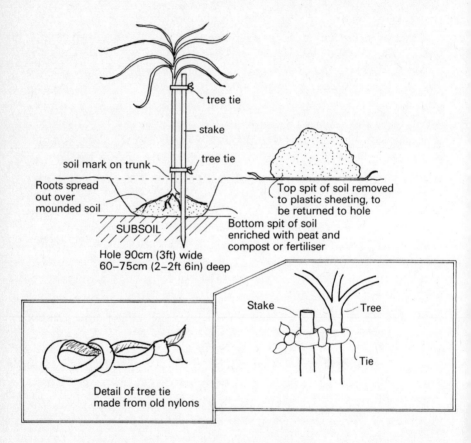

tree tie

stake

tree tie

soil mark on trunk

Roots spread
out over
mounded soil

Top spit of soil removed
to plastic sheeting, to
be returned to hole

Bottom spit of soil
enriched with peat and
compost or fertiliser

SUBSOIL

Hole 90cm (3ft) wide
60–75cm (2–2ft 6in) deep

Stake

Tree

Tie

Detail of tree tie
made from old nylons

in the autumn before it cools down. Again, you could use news-paper, covered by some soil, compost, grass-cuttings, leaves (kept in place by wire-netting) or bark, if you can afford it. Keep the mulch just clear of the trunk.

As well as the Eucalypts, there are other trees that can look their best in groups; some fastigiates, the Silver Birches and several of the slim columnar Conifers come to mind; A group of three of these, planted at the end of some vista, however small (how small can a vista be before you bark your nose on the end of it?), could be just what you need; they would all look beautiful, in their own different ways, throughout the year.

Some of the weeping trees make wonderful scene-stealers, from the full-sized Weeping Willows and Beeches to the tiny *Cotoneaster hybridus pendulus*, the Kilmarnock Willow, the Caraganas and *Sophora* 'Pendula'. Quite a few shrubs can be trained to make small trees, by selecting a strong leader, tying this to a stake and pruning off the lower shoots. The standard rose 'Canary Bird' makes an effective centre-piece to a small bed, as does a *Buddleia alternifolia*.

As in all planting, there are several points to be taken into consideration before making your final choice. The first, of course, is to find a tree that appeals to you, preferably one that you can hardly bear to be without. That done, research feverishly to find out if it will be a 'good doer' in your soil and climate; it is particularly important in those trees that are to be the 'bones' of your plan. Will it obtain and remain a size that will fill but not overflow its allotted space? Will the tree blot out a view you wish to retain, or fail to hide an eyesore? Will it overhang the sunniest beds, take light from the windows or, even worse, will its greedy roots rob the soil or undermine the foundations? It will be kind to remember your neighbours: will the tree have any adverse effects on them? If you are tempted to ignore this, remember that two can play at that game and you might be the next victim.

The form and colour of the tree and its foliage at all seasons, the bonuses of blossom, scent, fruit and berries, all must be considered. Some have colorations that are lost in shady places; others will be at their finest there. Wind will scorch one, sun shrivel another. If the garden is so small that you must make do with only one tree, the nicety of your choice will be even more important. Do you choose one that combines several of the virtues, or another that is so outstanding in just one that all else is forgiven? Only you can decide, but quite often, this year's love is soon outgrown, its charm having palled with familiarity. Such, alas, is our fickle nature. It is best in these cases to make a clean break before the roots grow too deep; remove the poor reject to a quiet corner where it may mope for a while and then, with luck, recover, like an abandoned mistress, pensioned off to the back streets of Fulham.

Next comes the infilling with further trees and shrubs. Ideally, a good proportion of these should retain their foliage all year long. This is even more important when your boundaries are more useful than beautiful, and in those parts of the garden that are visible from the house. At some distance, the tracery of bare

branches against a winter sky has much beauty, but a touch of greenery, a streak of gold or a soft blur of silver can give a great deal of comfort in the dreariest months when spring seems an unlikely dream. Some shrubs, such as the Senecios, look especially magical when rimed with frost, and should be placed where the sun can catch them and make them sparkle. All shades of green and gold, some blues, and silver, can be found in our gardens in winter, whilst one or two of the evergreens take on red overtones in the cold months. Other trees and shrubs, both evergreen and deciduous, come into flower between October and March, being especially valued for their bravery. Fruits, berries and coloured barks all add to the picture.

Unless you have plumped for a sophisticated planting scheme, involving not more than two colours—green and white, perhaps, or silver and blue (yes, yes, I know that white is not a colour)—it is pleasant to have a continuous succession of colours, blossoms and scents throughout the year and good economic sense to choose those plants that are willing to reproduce themselves freely in some way or another, whether by seeds, division or cuttings.

Some species are so anxious to survive that the merest twig of them, stuck into the ground in the most casual of fashions, or even by chance, will sprout away and grow into a tree before you can say 'boo'. Many a bean-pole or pea-stick has astonished the novice gardener (and probably the beans) by taking root and bursting into leaf. Willows are apt to do this and Forsythia will have a go, whilst many Roses grow well from these hardwood cuttings. Other plants simply droop into the earth and their tips take root there. Blackberries and their relations do this, while, in my garden, *Forsythia suspensa*, Winter Jasmine and various honeysuckles have obliged in this way.

A number of shrubs are so ready to perpetuate themselves that any healthy sprig from them can be stuck straight into reasonable soil, in a shaded spot, and a good proportion will root, although they would probably not be ungrateful if you stirred a bit of peat and sand into the cutting bed first. I have had successes this way with Choisyas, Hebes, Rue, Senecios, Lavender, Rosemary and many others. Of course, you are likely to get an even higher success rate if you do things more scientifically and prepare a proper seed-bed, either in the open ground or in containers and cold frames. The use of hormone rooting powders and some kind of glass or plastic cloches can also help. Still, the simplest methods take so little time that it is always worth giving them a go.

It is also worth accepting any offers of plant material whenever it is offered, even if this is not at the officially approved time of year. They may not be offered, or you may not be around to take them, when the so-called right time comes. Accept gratefully and hope for the best; with a bit of luck all will be well. Wrap the proffered material with damp tissues or newspaper and add a second wrapping of polythene. Thus protected, the offerings should survive if you get them home and dealt with as soon as possible.

If you have large areas to fill, do not be too choosy about your infilling to begin with. Plant what you can get free, cheaply or by propagation, which will fill up the space and keep the weeds down. As these have cost you little, it will be no great wrench to heave them out when you have found something a bit more choice to take their place. With any luck, you can trade these outcasts with someone else, donate them to a plant stall or, if all else fails, add them to the compost heap.

It is, in general, better to plant the smaller subjects in bold masses, groups of three, five or seven, punctuated here and there by the odd single specimen of striking appearance to provide a high note or exclamation mark. A billow of lavender sharpened by a standard rose 'Ballerina', perhaps, or some plump Choisyas in front of a fastigiate or cone-shaped tree. However, I do have a particular dislike of conifers popping up like importunate children, from island beds of heather—but then I do not care much for heather, except on the moors.

To this infilling of trees, shrubs and sub-shrubs you can add the finishing touches of herbaceous perennials, biennials, annuals, grasses and bulbs, all chosen on the same principles as the other plants. This is the merest theory, of course. One ends up, inevitably, with a curious mixture of bargains, cast-offs, and the fruits of love-at-first sight, which can be triumphs or disasters. Never mind, we plant and replant, lose the apples of our eye whilst the unrighteous flourish and make takeover bids, usually successful. Many herbaceous perennials grow swiftly and can be increased simply by division, so that you need only buy one plant at most, from which all others will be descended. Indeed, you should not have to buy *any* of the more common varieties if you have gardening friends, as they will be happy to donate their surplus material at division time. Many people are short of time or muscle to look after their gardens, and an offer of help with the autumn tidy-up in return for surplus plants could be accepted gratefully, especially by the elderly.

Unless you have a great deal of spare time and energy, I would not advise planting a traditional herbaceous border. Lovely as they are when seen at their best, they require endless attention to keep them looking that way. You will be forever about them, as the plants must be staked, divided, cut, sprayed, dusted and generally fussed over, while the more dedicated border-fanciers are hard at it, training late-flowering Clematis through early-flowering plants and early-flowering Clematis away from late-flowering plants, all the while whipping pots of Lilies and other bulbs into any odd corner and whizzing a procession of annuals through each bare patch where something has succumbed to pests or diseases. I feel quite pale just to think of it.

Better, I feel, to adopt the fashion, which has become deservedly popular, of mixing trees, shrubs, herbaceous plants and bulbs in a carefully controlled riot, preferring those plants which, being sturdy and promiscuous, will reward you with their offspring, some of whom may be so noteworthy that they become commercially desirable, in which case they may make you enough money to become a profligate gardener, rather than a penny-pincher.

You will often see island beds recommended, for ease of maintenance and the healthy growth of plants, which are not 'drawn up' by backing hedges, etc., but I hate the beastly things; they look like diseased kidneys floating round the garden. Have your borders away from a hedge if you must, but make them a pair of straight ones, edging a path or leading to a view. In any case, if you plant the taller subjects a foot or so away from the hedge, they should not be much trouble, and you can use the gap as an access path to service the border. It is quite a good idea to place stepping-stones through a large border for the same purpose.

So there it is: clear your land, dig it thoroughly, adding as much in the way of soil improvers as you can lay your hands on; then, having chosen your plants realistically, however you plan to come by them, get them into their designated spots, firm them in, staking if necessary, and water them sensibly, probably more often than you had imagined, for at least the first two years, keeping the weeds at bay and the soil mulched whenever possible. The aim will be to get all the earth covered by plants, but until that happy day comes, wage war on weeds by one method or another. A lot of plants, particularly alpines, will appreciate a handful of gravel below and about them at planting time. Bulbs, too, like some fine gravel or coarse grit to sit upon and many of the silver plants will feel at home with a top dressing about them, as will the Phormiums and a lot of other rather tender subjects. It also helps to discourage slugs, who, understandably enough, do not relish oozing across the rough surface of the stones.

If you should decide to go in for propagation, most gardening books have simple, easy-to-follow instructions and illustrations of the various techniques involved, while the section of the Royal Horticultural Society's *Encyclopaedia of Practical Gardening* which deals with plant propagation is invaluable, as indeed is the rest of the book. If you have a large garden, invest in it or borrow it from a friend. However, if I describe some of the simple ways, it may spur you on. Seeds are an obvious way to start. They are not too expensive, although the cost can mount up if you have a large flower and kitchen garden to stock. Your friends may supply you with some they have collected, or you can collect your own from the wild (not rare species, please) or from the plants that you already possess. Not all of them will come up and some that do will be disappointing, but you will have a good proportion of successes and maybe one or two pleasant surprises.

Seeds can be sown into composts sold as 'seed' or 'sowing' mixtures. A variety of free containers can be used. Plastic yoghourt pots, for instance, egg-boxes, plastic and polystyrene trays that have contained supermarket goodies, and a host of others. The advantages of using containers made from pulped paper (e.g. egg-boxes) or from thin cardboard, such as sections cut from old loo-rolls or tubing from foil and cling-film rolls, is that when the seeds have germinated, they can be planted out into the seed beds in their containers, without disturbance. The containers will rot down gently in the damp earth and the roots of the plants will be able to penetrate quite easily into the surrounding soil. It will help if you moisten the containers before putting them into the earth.

Some plants seed themselves so freely that all *you* have to do is let them get on with it, although you can give them a helping hand by shaking them over any bits of bare earth as you wander round the garden in the evenings, glass in hand. Cyclamen, Crocuses, Valerian, Forget-me-nots, Hellebores, Campanulas, Alchemilla, Honesty and many others spread themselves round my garden in this obliging fashion. It costs nothing and any surplus plants that result from all this fecundity can be given to friends, or swopped. You do have to hand-weed, of course, so that you do not accidentally destroy the little dears, and some of them that come up in an inconvenient place will have to be transplanted to more appropriate surroundings, but there will be many happy accidents and plant combinations that you would never have thought of. Some of these will be wild flowers that have arrived in a spirit of adventure and taken a liking to the local conditions. Many of them will get a welcome from me. *Corydalis lutea* is one of my favourite plants; its feathery leaves and engaging yellow flowers are cheerful all summer through. It pops up all over the place once it decides to stay with you, and it is quite capable of overpowering something small and self-effacing, so you will have to watch it. It pays to have a tough immigration policy with the wild bunch.

At other times and with other plants I am more careful. I watch them cunningly as the seed heads or pods develop. When they become ripe-looking, changing colour and texture, I tie a paper bag over their heads so that, if they should pop and spill their seeds when I am not looking, the paper bags will catch the little blighters. You can detach the heads, still in their bags, and hang them in a warm, dry place to finish drying out; shake the bags from time to time, so that the seeds fall out into the bottom of the bag, ready for you to collect and store them, carefully labelled, for sowing at the appropriate time. Poppies, Lupins, Sweet Peas, the Perennial Pea (*Lathyrus latifolius*) and Runner Beans are all easy ones to start with, but the seeds of the Sweet Pea and other legumes have tough seed-coats and it is often advisable to nick these with a razor-blade or rasp the coat with a file and then soak them for 12–24 hours before sowing.

Having gathered and prepared your seeds, take the pots or seed-trays and fill them to the brim with a suitable compost, levelling it off by pulling a piece of card or wood across the top of the container. Then, with another piece of card or wood, cut to fit, press the compost lightly and firmly so that it is about 1cm (½″) below the rim of the container. Sow the seeds as evenly as possible and not too thickly. If the seed is very fine, mix it with coarse sand or some tea-leaves, as this will make it easier to distribute satisfactorily. Cover the seeds with a little sieved compost to not more than their own thickness in most cases, then water them gently, using a can with a fine rose so that the seeds are not disarranged. It is a good idea to start the flow of water from the can away from the seed trays, then move it across the trays and away again, as this prevents the heavier drops of water that come at the beginning and end of the process from affecting the containers.

Cover the containers with a pane of glass wrapped in cling-film and a piece of folded newspaper. Place the seed-trays in a warm, dark place, if you have one, such as an airing cupboard, at a

temperature of about 70°F. As soon as the seeds have germinated, remove the glass and put the seeds in a light place but out of direct sunlight which could scorch and shrivel them. A conservatory, glassed-in porch or light window-sill would do. If you have no interior window-sills, fix up some kind of shelving across a light window. Of course, if you have a greenhouse of any kind, even one of the miniature lean-to variety, with sliding doors, you will increase your capacity for seedlings, etc., no end. They can be insulated quite cheaply with sheets of bubble plastic. The seedlings will need gentle watering or spraying as well as regular sprays with fungicides to prevent disease. As soon as they are large enough to handle easily (by the leaves, not the stems), they should be potted on into individual containers and gradually hardened off by being placed outside in a sheltered spot or a cold frame until they are sturdy enough to be planted out when all danger of frosts has passed.

A cold frame is a useful thing to have if there is enough space for one. It can be used for sowing the hardier seeds, rooting cuttings, hardening off plants and over-wintering treasures of doubtful hardiness. It can be made from all the usual 'free' materials —bricks, blocks and timber—or even by making walls of cut turves, which would make a snug shelter. 120cm (4ft) long by 90cm (3ft) wide is a good size, but this will probably be determined by the size of the cover you can find. It is often possible to pick up an old window-frame, complete with glass, from demolition sites or from properties that are being renovated. You may have to 'buy a drink', as it is delicately put, for the foreman, but it will make an excellent top for your frame. It can be propped up by a brick or bit of timber to ventilate the frame when necessary. Other tops can be made from plastic nailed to battens or from sheets of corrugated plastic. Remember to give your frame a gentle slope from about 30cm (1ft) at the back to 23cm (9″) at the front, so that rain is allowed to run off. The frames can be covered with off-cuts of carpet or old door mats for extra insulation in frosty weather.

If you have no room for a cold frame, you might be able to

accommodate a cloche or two. These little tents of glass or plastic can warm up the soil before sowing seed in the open ground, bring on the plants early and give protection from wind, rain and predators. They can be bought quite reasonably or you can make your own, of course; construct a tent-shaped frame of battens or stiff wire (opened-out coat-hangers are good) and fix panes of glass or pieces of plastic to this frame. Then make two hoops of wire to fit over the cloche and go on down into the ground to anchor it, as the winds delight in lifting cloches and tossing them about the garden, which can cause quite a lot of damage. Once again, opened out coat-hangers will do the job. Extra pieces of glass or rigid plastic can be placed over the open ends of the cloches when necessary. In the summer, you can remove the glass and tack on some plastic netting or old net curtaining which will let in the sun and rain but keep off birds, cats and the worst of the winds. As well as these tent-cloches, you can make bell-jars from large glass jars, such as the catering-sized pickled onion bottles (ask the pub to save you some) or from large plastic bottles—the jumbo Coke and lemonade kind or plastic sweet-shop jars. Saw or knock off the bottom of these containers and place them over your treasures. The screw-tops can be left on or removed to suit your purposes. Those little plastic domes which are supposed to keep flies off the food can also be used, and so can the small net umbrellas, designed for the same purpose; they, too, can be placed over individual plants such as strawberries, to keep off birds, etc. Both the domes and the umbrellas can be bought cheaply enough and often turn up at jumble sales and similar venues.

Those invaluable coat-hangers can be used in other ways: just form two of them into hoops and place these, one above the other, at right-angles over a plant to save it from accidental damage. If you then put a clear plastic bag over the hoops and fix it with wire or elastic bands, you have another form of mini-cloche. The hangers can be straightened out and used as canes, but remember to push a cork or empty pill bottle over the tops of them, so that you do not leave an eye or two impaled when rootling about in the border.

This is a sensible precaution for all canes and stakes; I have lost count of the injuries that I have sustained from wicked slithers of bamboo, stumbled upon incautiously. Alternatively, you can pull the hangers into a diamond-shape or circle; then straighten out the hook and push this into the top of a bamboo cane, thus forming a support for floppy herbaceous plants. The cane can be raised gradually as the plants grow up through the hoop. Of course, you could always leave the hangers as they are and wire bunches of herbs, flowers and seed heads on to them to dry in an airing cupboard. Once you get addicted to wire hangers, there will be no end to your ingenuity.

But back to the business of filling the garden. If some of your seeds fail to germinate, it could be that they are of the type that needs to be subjected to frost to break its dormancy. Place the seed trays outside in a light place out of direct sunlight. Cover them with a pane of glass until after Christmas, then remove the glass and leave the cold weather to get at them. Some seeds will take at least two years to germinate in this way, so do not despair and chuck the compost out. This process is known as stratification, but do not let that put you off. Seeds from Lilies, Paeonies, Hellebores and Hollies seem to enjoy this cold comfort. A little extra sand in the compost and a layer of grit over it helps to keep the drainage going. Some fleshy seeds, such as those of Lilies, do not like being dried out and should be sown into the compost straight from the matured seed head.

Spurred on by your success (I hope) with seeds, you might try your hand at cuttings next. The easiest of all are those where you just thrust a twig or sprig into a jar of water and wait for roots to develop. Put a piece of thick paper or thin card over the glass and make a hole for the stem to go through. Remove all leaves from the bottom half of the stem and push it through the card which will support the sprig. The bottom half of the stem should be well down into the water, which you will have to top up from time to time. Place the glass on a light window-sill and, in time, small white roots, like linen thread, will sprout from the bottom of the twig and

SUPPORTS AND CLOCHES

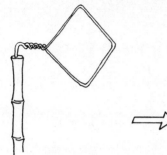

Opened-out coat hanger
stuck into bamboo cane
as a plant support

Tent cloche frame and . . .

. . . wire hoops to keep it in
place, made from coat hangers

Plastic sweet jar or
glass pickled onion jar
with bottom removed,
used as cloche

Cutting in container
placed in inflated plastic
bag. Twigs inserted into
compost to keep plastic
away from cutting

fill up the whole glass if you leave it there long enough. Then the rooted twig can be potted up and allowed to grow on. This is always the tricky part. You will need a light, open compost with lots of peat and sand or perlite. I would pop a plastic bag over the potted-up plant, blowing into it to inflate it, and then seal the top with a tie or rubber band. A few small sticks or wire hoops placed over the plant before you put it in the bag will help to keep it clear of the plastic. A week or two in this should give the plant a good start, and then you can cut a corner of the bag away to let in a little air, before removing the bag and allowing the plant to make it unaided. Ivies, Skimmias, Hebes and Privet are among the plants that root easily in water. As it is such a simple method, you can try a sprig of anything you fancy and see what happens. There are now some rooting gels on the market, of which I have heard good reports; they are used in the same fashion.

The plastic-bag-inflated-over-a-pot of compost can be used just as well to propagate soft or half-ripe cuttings, while the latter can also be placed in a sheltered cutting bed. For this, make a simple timber frame or knock the bottom out of a wooden box or crate. Place this directly onto the ground, out of direct sunlight. Half fill this box with a commercial cutting compost or make your own from equal quantities of peat and sand. Make little planting holes in the compost with a pencil or similar tool. Prepare your cuttings, which you have taken with a sharp knife, by removing the bottom leaves and keeping only about two pairs of leaves at the top. Dip the bottom of the stem in water and then into hormone rooting powder, shaking off any surplus. Place the cuttings into the planting holes and firm them in gently. Water them and cover with glass or plastic. It is a good precaution to add some fungicide to the can when watering, and keep this up in future waterings, if and when these become necessary. Not all your cuttings will take, but you should get enough to encourage you to carry on.

Hardwood cuttings are even simpler. You can take them at leaf fall, about 15–25cm (6″–10″) long. Most of the cutting should be buried in the open ground, but leave about three buds above the surface. The top of the stem is also cut off. If you like, you can use a little hormone rooting powder for the more difficult subjects, but many will be only too eager to survive without any such cosseting. You should dig over the soil where you plan to put the cuttings and, again, this should be out of direct sunlight. If the ground is heavy, add a little sand and peat to the trench. Firm the cuttings into the soil and remember to check them after any frosts. You may have to firm them again if they have been lifted.

Some plants can be increased by layering, that is by pinning one or two of their runners or branches into the soil and weighting them down with a stone, or fixing them into position with wire pegs—hairpins for the smaller plants and those coat-hangers again for the toughies. Prepare the soil by adding some peat and sand. You can fill a pot with this mixture and sink it up to its rim in the soil, layering into this, so that when roots have formed and the plant can be severed from its parent, it can be moved without disturbance. The layering is usually taken near the tip of the branch which is nicked on the underside, and if necessary, dipped into rooting powder. Bend the branch sharply upwards and bury the joint about 10–15cm (4″–6″) in the soil. Pin or weight it into position and keep the soil watered when necessary. When the plant puts out new leaves in the following year you will know it has rooted. Wait until autumn before severing the new plant but leave it in place for a few weeks. Then cut off the tip to encourage it to branch out a bit before potting up or planting out. This whole process can take up to two years with some subjects.

Finally, have a go at increasing your Lily stock by growing on the offsets which form either just above or just below some Lily bulbs, and also the bulbils that develop in the leaf axils of others. Collect these when they are mature and plant them, in pots or seed trays, in a John Innes No.1 compost, covering them with grit. Top them with glass or put them in a cold frame for about 12 months before potting up or planting out. Bulbs can also be increased from scales, if they have them. Remove a few of the outer scales and place them in a bag containing some fungicidal powder, shaking the bag until the scales are coated thoroughly. Mix up equal amounts of moist peat and grit, add the scales and put the lot into a polythene bag which you then inflate by blowing into it and tying it firmly at the neck. Label the bag and place it in an airing cupboard or similar snug. After about six weeks or so, small bulblets should appear at the base of the scales. When this happens, bury each scale, complete with its bulblets, into a pot containing potting compost so that just the tip of the scale is visible, cover with grit and water gently. Keep in a warm, light place until the bulbs produce their spring leaves. Harden the plants off and, when the leaves die down that autumn, lift and plant each new bulb into a pot. Whichever way you use to grow new Lilies, they will need protection from slugs.

I hope this has whetted your appetite for more. These are just the merest basics of propagation. It is a complicated and fascinating, not to say rewarding pastime. Do read Christopher Lloyd's *The Well-Tempered Garden* for his observations on the subject; indeed, he is indispensable reading for any self-respecting gardener, telling, as he does, what the text-books leave out and passing on the knowledge gained by his wide experience in an immensely readable way, so that you will find you have learnt a lot of lessons in an entirely painless fashion.

I would just remind you that you should use all the walls of your house to add extra space for plants. Many rather tender species will only survive if given the warmth of a wall to succour them. There are suitable plants to grow on walls of any aspect and it will be a very remarkable house indeed that is not improved by some well-chosen ones clambering about its person. Another thing. . . . In this country fig trees will be particularly grateful for a south-facing wall behind them. They like their roots confined; I have heard it suggested that they should be planted in the belly of a dead pig or, failing that, a Gladstone bag, but I think a large pot, sunk to its rim, would do nicely, or you could build them a something comforting below ground from bricks or slabs . . . I just threw that in to make things more interesting . . .

One final bit of advice: plant a few giants that will give an awful lot of *pow* to your garden. They will fill up yards of space quickly, which can only be an economy, and they will rescue you from a boring neatness and timidity. Try the larger Artemisias, Lavatera, *Crambe cordifolia*, Gunneras, Rheums, et al.

7   FOLLY DE GRANDEUR

Ornaments and furniture

I have touched on the subject of garden ornaments in the previous chapters but propose to explore it a little more thoroughly here, with a brief foray into garden furniture. I suppose that ornament in the garden could be divided roughly into three basic types: dignified restraint, cheerful vulgarity and over-the-top fantasy. To the first category belong urns, obelisks, genuine classical statuary, pillars, balustrades and similar conceits. Gnomes, plastic windmills, cement cats with blue-glass eyes, bare-bottomed children and bloated concrete putti, thatched 'well-heads', reproduction street-lamps in crazy-paving patios—all these belong, with many other jollities, in the middle group; while the last collection would have tropical murals, classical *trompe l'oeil* vistas, the wilder flights of topiary, and pavilions and follies of every sort, and from every culture.

For the purposes of this book, I shall ignore the middle group; if you love such things, they are not that expensive; you can even obtain a mould in which to make your own gnomes, and every probable and improbable object can be used as either container or ornament; exuberance rules . . .

If, on the other hand, you feel that dignified restraint is absolutely *you*, ingenuity will have to be tempered by refinement. Simplicity will be the most important factor to consider and this will certainly be cost-effective. Ornamental features can be 'soft' or 'hard'; that is, from growing plants or from construction materials. Two plain clay pots, placed on either side of the front door and containing a mop-headed standard or an obelisk of Ivy, trained up supporting canes, would be a delightful combination of both, and

not expensive if you grow and train the plants yourself. A mop-
headed Bay or Box tree is a wickedly expensive luxury to buy, or to
receive as a special present; but a jolly little standard of golden
Privet that you have trained yourself is within everyone's budget,
especially if you have grown it from a free cutting or hedge-
trimming (and these are often found lying around on the pavements). Ivy, too, is easy to grow from cuttings and layerings, so
that all you need is time and patience. If you have space to take
evergreen cuttings, there is no end to the number of green, silver
and gold 'ornaments' that you can grow; cones, obelisks, squares,
balls, diamonds and every variety of creature can be trained and
clipped into shape. Yew, Box, Lonicera and Privet will be suitable
for this kind of sculpture, while almost anything can be trained
as a weeping standard or a mop-head. Fuschias, some Roses,
Buddleias, Brooms, etc., make good weepers, while Bay, Eleagnus,
Euonymus, Daisies, other Roses and a host of plants can be
trained into mop-heads. Any plant material which you can obtain
for nothing, or for very little cash, would be worth experimenting
with.

One jolly ruse that you could try is to wind the shoot of a pliant
climber round a cane or stake until it hardens into maturity and will
keep its barley-sugar shape when the support is withdrawn.
Remove all side-shoots that grow on the twisted portion of the
stem and allow the shoots at the top to develop into a weeper or a
mop-head, according to type of plant. Wistarias look wonderful
like this and Honeysuckle is an easy one. I see no real reason why
any reasonably resilient climber could not be treated in this way.
As you need a young plant to train, material that you have
propagated will be ideal and free. Young plants are cheaper to buy
than large specimens, so would not be likely to upset the budget.
For obelisks and cone shapes, etc., plants can be trained over a
framework of canes and wire, or battens and netting, into a dense,
glittering surface. Nothing gives a young garden more of an instant
'lift' than these high-spots.

Other plants are so striking in their natural state that they need

SUPPORTS FOR CLIMBERS

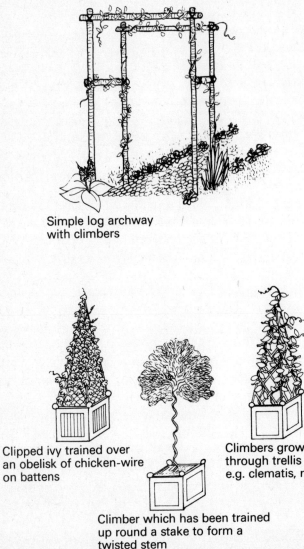

Simple log archway
with climbers

Clipped ivy trained over
an obelisk of chicken-wire
on battens

Climber which has been trained
up round a stake to form a
twisted stem

Climbers growing up and
through trellis obelisk,
e.g. clematis, runner beans, etc.

nothing but the simplest of containers to set them off, and thus become an ornament in themselves. These are the so-called 'architectural' plants, and very fashionable, too. They are usually evergreen or whatever else keeps its foliage throughout the year, although sometimes a deciduous plant has such attractive foliage in the summer and interestingly shaped branches in winter that it would qualify for inclusion. Some of the Japanese Maples and the small Crab-Apples that hold their fruit in winter are possible choices. The evergreens include Magnolias, Fatsias, Yuccas, Phormiums, Palms, Bamboos and the larger Euphorbias. Once again, the humble Privet can be a cheap and excellent choice. It has many forms, as well as the familiar green or gold hedgers. There are gold, silver and cream variegations, some of them just flushed with pink; whilst others have such large glossy leaves that you could mistake them for Camellias, and carry heavy heads of cream flowers with a distinctive scent which I love, although others give it some very rude epithets.

My eldest daughter has just moved into a village house in Hampshire, whose previous owner had gardened there from the beginning of the century. Her garden is eccentric and magical. She must have been the salvager of all time. It is a coastal village, and lengths of rope and chain, which have an obviously nautical origin, have been looped around the garden from trees and posts. Along these loops grow festoons of Wistaria and Ivy, forming boundaries and arbours in the most delightful fashion. It is an idea which could be copied by anyone, in a formal or informal way. If you are faced with a blank wall, one or two of a large variety of climbers could be trained over it in a formal pattern—in diamonds, circles and loops or whatever you could dream up. Both self-clingers and others that need support could be used for this. Both would need careful shaping and clipping, of course, but an easier shape would be some kind of arch. This could frame a view (real or painted), a mirror to give the illusion of gardens beyond, or some kind of statue or urn.

Of course, you could construct a genuine arch against the wall,

either of brickwork, timbers or wire. The latter could be made for you by a blacksmith or bought from a garden centre, but would be rather tricky to make yourself, whereas those in brick or timber should be quite simple for any but the most cack-handed. Your arch could be square (can one have a square arch?), round or Gothic. Over the arch could be trained all the usual climbers: Roses, Ivies, Honeysuckles, Jasmines, Hops, even Runner Beans (*another* economic double for you), and too many others to name.

All sorts of arbours and pavilions could be made in roughly similar ways. Simplest of all are those made against a wall, and of these the easiest is that made across a corner. Here you will need only one piece of timber, or whatever, placed across the corner to form a seat, with two pieces of timber to support it screwed to the walls, or you could rest this triangular-shaped seat on a brick pier. Another, similar, construction is fixed to form a roof. It could be made lattice-fashion, through which climbers could dangle to offer dappled shade; or solid, in which case it should be set at a slight slope and waterproofed: with roofing felt, perhaps, or paint; possibly with tiles and slates if you are a little more ambitious. Even plastic, tacked to battens, would do, if you smothered it with an evergreen climber.

Against a flat wall, of course, your structure would need sides as well as a top of some kind. The sides could be made from bricks, blocks or timber—perhaps a combination of all three—either solid or trellised in some manner. It really does not matter if you make a hash of it, as the kindly plants will disguise your errors. In fact you can make a rather pleasant little hideout just from the plants, without the need to construct a frame for them. Flesh out the walls with evergreens/golds that will take to being clipped. Train them with bamboo canes and wire to branch out until the walls are solid (with perhaps a window or two), and up and over to form a roof of some sort.

With free-standing pavilions and gazebos, things are a bit more complicated. You will need four walls as well as a top. If it is for ornament only, the top can be omitted or at least reduced to a mere suggestion. If you took the course in bricklaying that I suggested *and* haunted enough demolition sites, you could, I suppose, make a real folly; all ruined towers and fallen arches, if you know what I mean. If not, something much simpler will be in order. Any four posts stuck into the ground can form the basis of a pavilion or gazebo. Be a little more ambitious and use eight posts, thus forming (surprise, surprise) an octaganol. To this basic shape you can attach trellis, or some oriental panels, rustic logs . . . whatever. Bamboos, chains, ropes, wires, etc., could all be used and your less successful efforts could, as always, be smothered with greenery. You may find abandoned scaffolding-poles lying about your garden when you move in, and these, along with stripped-out iron gas pipes, etc., can be used as uprights for pavilions and pergolas,

FOLLIES DE GRANDEUR

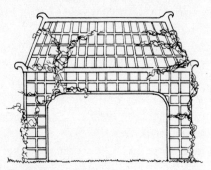

Garden house of timber frame and trellis sides, with Victorian roof finials

6 or 8 sided pavilion from timber and ply, wooden finials on roof, 'tiles' cut from roofing felt nailed on battens

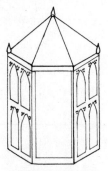

Garden pavilion from timber and ply with curtain rail finials

Arbour of four posts and four rafters covered with climbers

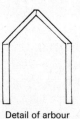

Detail of arbour

topped with lengths of timber. Pergolas can be made entirely of timber, of course, including rustic logs. These can look a bit twee, but if you make them sturdily enough this can be avoided.

If you are stuck with an indispensable but uninviting garden shed, you might consider transforming it into something a little more fanciful. Using off-cuts of plywood and some beading, the windows can be given a Gothic look. Add Strawberry Hill crenellations and roof-finials, paint it white or a subtle colour, grow a climber over it and place a pair of standard or cone-shaped trees in pots on either side of the door; a veritable transformation, as Poirot might have said. This trick with plywood arches and beading can be used to make your garden-door more exciting, too. Cut two pieces of plywood into identical half-arches. These can be fixed in place over the existing square or oblong panes of glass, using either panel pins, beading or Araldite. If you use glue it will be necessary to repeat the arches on both sides of the glass, to hide the glue. If you do not have the skill to cut the plywood, paint the arches and glazing-bars directly onto the glass.

Should you come across some old or 'bargain-offer' louvred shutters, these can be pressed into service to make the sides of your arbours, as indeed can sections cut from pensioned-off ladders. For the children's garden, you could construct a log cabin and a palisade from branches or odds and ends of timber.

Shops, TV and film studios often make elaborate structures for their windows and sets. If you make friends with the window-dressers and the studio staff, you may be able to obtain some of their cast-offs, which are often thrown away or smashed up. Exhibitions would be another place to look. Talk to the staff on the stands and find out what is going to happen to the display when the show is over. You may find buildings, fencing, trellises, pillars, pools and statues from these sources; many of them would need to be disguised a bit, but they could save you a deal of construction work, particularly if you have decided on a fantastical approach. Imagine a Doric pillar, swathed with Ivy in a carefully framed corner of your garden. Weather-stained, (helped by a liberal

TRANSFORMING A PANEL DOOR

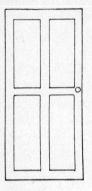

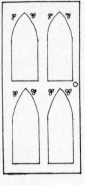

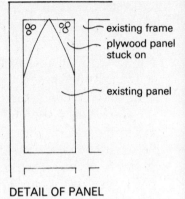

existing frame

plywood panel stuck on

existing panel

BEFORE

AFTER

DETAIL OF PANEL

TRANSFORMING A GARDEN SHED

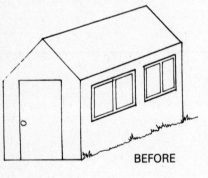

BEFORE

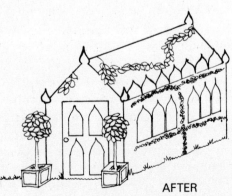

AFTER

application of liquid manure), who would know that it had started life in a shop window?

As for the 'hard' ornaments, any number of them can be made from all the usual materials. I am not sure that you could manufacture an urn, although I suppose you could manage to take a cast of one and make copies in cement. In fact it is easy enough to buy cement urns very cheaply. The shapes are not at all bad, but the texture has a drear, dead look, so you will have to improve them with a little paint or stain them down with liquid manure. It is amazing how much a few coats of liquid manure can improve anything made of cement. Not only do they begin to look like natural stone, but mosses and lichens are encouraged to grow on them, thus completing the illusion. By the time you have grown a few trailers in and over them, it is difficult to tell them from the genuine article, even close up.

You will certainly be able to make a plinth for your urns or statues, either from bricks, (plain or rendered) or from timber. A simple one is made from a wooden box, either square or oblong. Nail chicken-wire to the outside and make a stiff sand, cement and peat mixture (1:1:2), adding some Unibond to the mixing water. Then paint the box and the wire with more Unibond and apply the cement mixture with a trowel, smoothing it over the top and sides of the box, about 1–2cm (½"–¾") thick. When this has 'gone off', it can be painted with liquid manure, applying it coat by coat, and allowing it to dry out between coats until it is the right shade and resembles stone.

All sorts of containers can be covered in this fashion: jars, pitchers, bowls, etc; for them, omit the wire but rough up the surface a bit if possible, and paint with Unibond as above. This will turn quite flimsy indoor containers into something rugged and appropriate to outdoor use. The same technique can be used to turn rather beastly little cement statues into something more original, roughing up the surface a little with your fingers to give a look of genuine modern sculpture. The original statue will provide the armature or frame, on which you can create your own fancies.

You may be lucky enough to find some containers that are strong and striking enough in their own right to stand outside as they are, but unless you know they are frost-proof, bring them in during cold weather, or at least make sure they do not fill up with water which could freeze, expand and crack them or break them up.

There are a number of natural objects that can be used ornamentally in the garden, as I described in the chapter on water gardening. Logs, twisted roots, driftwood, mossy or lichened branches, stones, rocks, boulders, shells, even skulls. If you do not care for the idea of a sheep or cow's skull as an *object trouvé*, use them, once again, as an armature for an unusual sculpture. In addition to the natural objects, you could find all manner of ancient artefacts, whether industrial, agricultural or horticultural; a cog-wheel, plough-share or rusty lawn-roller would all serve, without being twee, although that is always something to watch. I suppose the first person to think of putting a ship's lantern or a pair of carriage-lamps outside his door would have been delighted with the originality of the concept.

Furniture is another matter altogether. You would have to be quite skilful to make serious furniture in the classical mould. You might be able to mock up something that would look splendid, but would it bear you up? Better to make something of supreme simplicity. Two piers of brickwork could support a flagstone for a seat, a slab of slate or marble for a table. Even simpler, get a couple of decorator's trestles, top them with a flush door or piece of chipboard and cover it with a cloth big enough to reach the ground. Bedcovers bought from Oxfam shops or jumble sales would fit the bill here and you could dye them in stunning colours to set off the china and your overall colour-scheme. This has the advantage that it can all be dismantled and put away when not in use, thus leaving the terrace free for sunbathing or skate-boarding, perhaps both together—why not?

The sewing-machine stand, topped with washstand marble, is now so familiar that it has become a cliché. If you are stuck with one, paint it anything but white, to make it a little less obvious. (But

ORNAMENTS

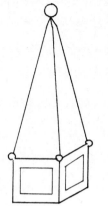

Painted
timber
obelisk

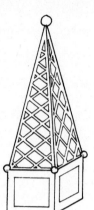

Painted obelisk
of trellis
and ply

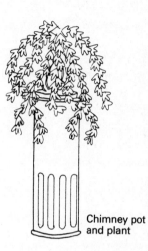

Chimney pot
and plant

Bricks, slabs
and pot

Rendered bricks
or blocks, slabs
and urn

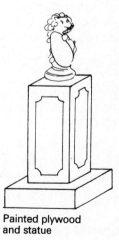

Painted plywood
and statue

Octangular
brick plinth
with slabs
and bowl

it did make a jolly good table). For fanciful or less formal schemes, all sorts of junk shop furniture can be stripped and painted, or stripped and varnished for garden use. It was possible to buy Lloyd-loom stuff for pennies a few years ago; when painted afresh and given a cushion or two, they made good garden chairs, but now they cost a fortune. Odd bits of Victorian and Edwardian bamboo furniture can occasionally be found quite reasonably and this looks good in the garden. If you buy one of the books on paint finishes, or attend one of those courses I keep going on about, you can turn your junk finds into fantasy objects, by marbling, tortoiseshelling, stippling, ragging, bambooing, graining and stencilling. The same paint finishes can be used on the ornamental objects that you made out of plywood: a marbled obelisk, a stippled plinth, etc.

Country auctions and the sort of junk shops that proclaim 'houses cleared' will sometimes provide you with ornaments and furniture, and remember to scan the small ads in the local papers and *Exchange and Mart*, and the postcards in local shops, which can also be a merry hunting-ground.

In the rustic garden, logs or sections of them, either on their own or combined with planks and slabs, will make the most basic but perfectly adequate seats, benches and tables. I suspect you have got the hang of things by now . . . Oh, I forgot, if you do plan to make a weeping standard from a Wistaria or something similar, you may need some kind of dome-shaped frame to train the branches over initially; use an upturned hanging basket for the smaller subjects and a dilapidated umbrella-frame for larger ones. This latter can be mended and strengthened with stiff wire, and they can both be lashed to a cane or stake with more wire.

8 GOING TO POT

Container gardening

Probably all gardeners, even those with several acres at their disposal, indulge in some form of container gardening, whether it be a row of antique urns, overflowing with extravagant bedding plants, a cheerful window-box or just a humble pot of herbs by the kitchen door. Containers have many charms and advantages; for the economical gardener, not the least of these will be their adaptability. They can go with you when you move on, can be trundled from sun to shade, raised on pedestals or sunk into the ground. Stand them in splendid isolation or huddle them in a friendly group; they can be grand or simple, ancient or modern, all things to all gardeners, in fact. They do have a few snags, it is true, needing as they do, to be watered frequently; while, on the other hand, they will quickly become waterlogged if you have not given them sufficient drainage. Ideally, their compost should be changed every couple of years or so, and many plants will come to resent having their roots restricted after a while, and sulk a bit. Some containers may be damaged by frost, whilst all but the smallest are heavy to manoeuvre, once filled and planted up. However, even with these drawbacks, most of us find them invaluable for all sorts of places and all kinds of use. For the purposes of this chapter, I shall include raised beds and pools.

Some of us, of course, will have no choice in the matter; it will be containers or nothing, and we may have space for little more than a window-box or a tub by the front door. For others who, for one reason or another, are seldom long in the same place, it will make sense to have their garden portable, while for the elderly and the handicapped, gardening in containers and raised beds may be the only possible solution. As I mentioned in Chapter 6, containers provide us with an easy way to grow those plants which have special requirements not met by the soil in the rest of the garden. Rampant growers can be kept in solitary confinement and the more tender creatures can be coddled and moved to sheltered spots when the weather worsens. Moreover, those of us who, like those irritating virgins, think to the future, can plant up a range of pot-grown beauties and keep them lurking about in some secluded spot until they are in full fig and can be popped into any bare spot or lack-lustre corner, there to provide an instant face-lift—much to the chagrin of the less provident.

Choose your containers with care. They should be robust enough to survive our winters and the odd knock from the unwary. They should be large and deep enough to provide sustenance to whatever you plant in them, and they should not be wildly out of keeping with their surroundings unless you tend towards the bizarre in these matters. Few of us will be lucky enough to possess the aristocrats of the container world: stone troughs and urns, lead cisterns, Versailles 'caisses' and large hand-thrown pots of Italian terracotta. Those of us who *are* so fortunate will have to be particularly careful when adding anything of a humbler kind, as the defects of these will become rather obvious in the presence of the grandees. However, you might not *need* to add anything more, as the impact of just one of these special fellows can be so great that they will be all the better when seen in solitary splendour. Use your spare cash (ha! ha!) to keep them positively bursting with the best possible plants, rather than surround them with their social inferiors.

For the rest of us, the choice is wide, and whether we buy the cheaper range of purpose-built containers, construct our own or use some ingenuity to adapt whatever we can lay our hands on, a lot can be achieved for a quite modest outlay.

Not for us, therefore, the most expensive of the purpose-made containers; the Versailles tubs of wood and fibreglass—in fact *anything* made of fibreglass will probably be beyond our budget, although we might save up for just one, I suppose. The most 'exclusive' (I love that word, don't you?) ranges of reconstituted stone would also be too pricey and so would be the larger of the imported terracotta pots. There are some very attractive glazed pots and containers of oriental origin around these days. The prices vary a great deal, but some of them are really not expensive for what they are, so shop around to find the bargains. In the middle price-range are a number of pots and troughs made from a variety of cement and concrete mixes. These are not to be despised as they are strong (if rather heavy) and the best of them look good either painted or left in their own neutral colours. Others can be given a coat or two of liquid manure which 'weathers' them down, and when given a trailing plant or two to soften them up a bit, they can look very like natural stone. It is usually best to choose those that have the simplest design, avoiding anything with swags and cherubs or mock Saxon carvings. Then come the cheaper wooden containers and window-boxes, tubs, machine-turned clay pots and containers of plastic and polystyrene. The last two are seldom very attractive for outdoor use, but they are light to move around and can be painted to match their surroundings or given 'hides' of rescued materials. Alternatively, they can be placed inside other, more attractive containers to be changed, throughout the season, as plants come and go. Of course, if you could plant them so thickly that they were positively smothered in greenery, you would be able to forget about their appearance when naked.

It is amazing what you can find in builder's yards—all sorts of construction materials that can be used for unusual containers: hollow concrete blocks, sections of drain-pipe and, indeed, many plumbing and draining components, some of them in most attractive glazed stoneware; plastic and metal water-tanks, of course, which are particularly useful for larger plants and pools; sturdy builder's buckets which are often to be found 'on offer'; plus a host of other possibilities. Often there are cracked or broken things lying around in odd corners and these may, if you ask nicely, be yours for little or nothing. They can usually be mended with something like Unibond, and the joins hidden by a cunning bit of positioning or planting. Of course, you might pick up any of these things on skips or demolition sites, while, if you are on friendly terms with your plumber, he might find some odds and ends for you and even a discarded sink or two, which you could leave as they are, paint, or cover with a mock hypertufa mixture. To do this, wash the sink thoroughly with a strong detergent and hot water. Scour the surface and apply a coat of Unibond. Then mix up sand, cement and peat (1:1:2) and mix with a little water to a strong, smooth sludge. Trowel this over the prepared sink to about 1–2cm (½"–¾") thick. As this mixture starts to harden, use your finger-tips or thumbs to give it a mildly dimpled texture that will resemble hewn stone. Cover with a damp sack or some such, so that it does not 'go off' too quickly. When it is completely hard, give the sink a couple of coats of liquid manure to 'weather' it and encourage the growth of mosses and lichens to complete its transformation.

If there is a pottery in your neighbourhood, visit it regularly to pick up any 'seconds' that you can persuade them to sell at bargain prices. These can be strengthened if necessary by giving them a cement rendering on the inside, using Unibond both as a preparatory coat and mixed into the rendering. A container that is slightly cracked can have its life extended by tying a length or two of strong galvanised wire round it at strategic points; the wire can be painted to match the container or hidden by plants.

Wooden tubs and casks are also to be found at very reasonable prices. Keep your eyes open in the garden centres and green-grocers' shops, as well as scanning local advertisments for them. They should be cleaned out thoroughly and given a coat or two of non-toxic preservative both inside and out, while the metal bands will last longer if you keep them painted.

Apart from demolition yards and skips, junk shops, jumble sales and all the other glory-holes I *keep* rambling on about will be happy hunting-grounds for all sorts of cheap containers. Coal-scuttles, watering-cans, tin and wooden trunks and hat-boxes, hods, baths and wash-tubs, pots, pans, jars, jugs and bowls of all descriptions will turn up from time to time and can be used. Do not go with pre-conceived ideas as to what is and what is not a container. Indulge in a little lateral thinking. In a cottage garden almost anything can be used and often is. A tin hat makes a hanging basket, ancient lavatories are flushed with Geraniums, an abandoned dinghy is awash with Petunias and a black firegrate is blazing with Nasturtiums. Two or three white-painted car tyres make a tub and another is a sandpit. Even logs can be chiselled out and planted up.

In formal surroundings you will have to show a little more restraint. It is not difficult to make containers from wood. Unless you are going for a rugged, rustic look, you will need planed timber, bought cut to size if necessary, but found easily enough in all the usual places. Hardwood is ideal, but you are more likely to find softwood and this will do well enough if it is stained or painted on the outside and brushed with preservative inside. Plastic can also be stuck to the inside, by way of a liner, but remember to pierce some holes through it for drainage. Wooden containers are best raised off the ground in some way to prevent the base from rotting. This can be done by screwing two wooden runners to the base or by propping the container up on some bricks. If you do not wish to raise them up in this fashion, set them on a bed of gravel which will help a bit.

Simple square containers made from bricks, blocks or slabs on edge can be cemented together quite easily by anyone, and you could use a bag of ready-mix for small jobs like this. A little washing-up liquid squeezed into the mixing water will help things to go smoothly. 'Hides' for ugly but practical containers can be made from timber or bricks, etc., and there will be no need for a base, just four sides into which the inner container can be dropped. If you are using bricks and blocks you can lay them un-mortared, so that they can be easily dismantled and taken with you or moved to another spot. Honeycomb brickwork will eke out the bricks if necessary, as suggested for walls in Chapter 4. Sleepers, too,

EASY WOODEN CONTAINERS

Plain

Beading panels

Versaille

Diagonal slats

Diagonal 2

Plywood and
5cm x 5cm (2"x2")
top moulding

Gothic

Plywood, trellis
battens, ball feet

Plywood and
5cm x 5cm (2"x2")
uprights

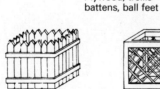

Picket

Trellis

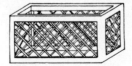

Hexagonal

Octagonal

Octagonal
tapered

can be piled up in this fashion, as their weight will keep them in place.

A more solid construction will be needed to make raised beds and pools, and unless you are building them on an already paved area, you will need to dig a trench for the foundations. They can be square, oblong, round, triangular, octagonal or what you will. They can be made singly or in a series of groups and terraces. Logs and unplaned timber will look right in country gardens, brick can be used anywhere, as can planed timber, while blocks and slabs on edge will look best in a modern setting unless they are spruced up with a facing of trellis, given a coping, perhaps, and painted sparkling white or some sophisticated shade of green instead. Beading and trellising can also be added to wooden containers and beds, or they can be given the Gothic touch. Having been so rude about concrete blocks in Chapter 4, I have to own up to finding some recently of a most attractive buff or honey colour with a pleasant texture. These would look splendid in the right place without any disguise whatsoever. Still, after all this, your cheapest choice for a raised bed will probably be salvaged bricks or timber. Whatever you use, do not forget to give the beds some weep-holes round the bottom, to improve the drainage. This is particularly important if the bed is set on a solid surface instead of open ground.

Some form of coping is always a neat finish to a raised bed and it provides a pleasant seat as well. This is particularly nice if you have made a raised pool, as happy hours can be spent just sitting and staring into the depths, which is very soothing indeed.

If there is a restaurant or delicatessen nearby, make friends with the owner or the staff, as quite often food is delivered to them in catering-sized packs of metal, wood or plastic that could be useful to you, either in their own right or as liners for something more decorative but fragile, like an old wicker basket. I once found some slim and elegant barrels outside a Chinese Restaurant. They were covered with the most intriguing symbols which led to a lot of useless speculation. These barrels made excellent containers as they gave a good depth of soil but did not take up much floor-room.

A lot of electrical equipment such as TV sets and stereo parts come packed in polystyrene boxes. These make very light containers which would be useful on roof gardens and balconies. They can be painted or treated in a similar fashion to that I described for re-vamping sinks. Coat the polystyrene with car underseal mastic and roll it in coarse sand, grit or ground stone. Larger sheets of polystyrene, from cookers, washing machines and refrigerators, etc., could be cut to size and stuck together with the stuff used to fix polystyrene tiles to the ceiling and then finished off as above. These containers could also be used to make a pool or a tray for children's water-play. Your local electrical retailer will probably be happy enough to get rid of them.

All sorts of metal containers can be used, from oil-drums at one end of the scale to paint-tins at the other. Remember that many metals are toxic, so it is sensible to give them all a couple of coats of bituminous or rubber paint on the inside to seal them and brush another couple of coats of ordinary paint of exterior quality on the outside to preserve the metal. If the containers are rusty, use one of the new products that combine with the rust to make a tough and rustproof undercoat. Your paint merchant will advise you about all these products.

The simpler metal containers, such as the above-mentioned oil-drums and paint-tins, can be given a pleasing uniformity by painting them all the same colour, either to match their surroundings if you want to 'lose' them, or in a strong colour if you want them to make a statement, as they say in Pseud's Corner. Alternatively, you could paint them every colour of the rainbow and a few others besides. This could look fun against a white wall and would be particularly jolly with the painted garden I described in Chapter 1. You could paint a rainbow in a blue sky on the wall behind them in case anyone had failed to get the idea. In a small area, these paint-tin containers could be hung aloft from different vantage points to give some instant height. Remember that plants that climb can also fall, so you can have one lot clambering up a trellis and another dangling down to embrace them, thus doubling the coverage rate.

Containers of china, earthenware and clay are usually ready to use straight away, but, like everything else, will need some drainage holes, which can be made by using a masonry bit on the slow speed of your drill. Place some masking tape across the part to be drilled to reduce the risk of cracks and splinters.

Whatever type of container you choose or have thrust upon you, the methods of filling them will be much the same, although the type of compost may vary. But for goodness sake play around with them for a while before you fill and plant them up, until you are sure that they are in the right place, as it is no fun humping any but the smallest ones when they are full. Apart from those holes that you are getting so bored with, they will need a minimum 5cm (2") layer of drainage material, except in the very small pots. It is quite a good idea to put something over the holes and under the drainage layer to keep the holes from becoming blocked, minimise the amount of soil washed away and to prevent a variety of nasties from creeping up for a cozy rest. Perforated zinc does the job well, and you can also use hessian or nylon curtains, or a pair of laddered tights could be crumpled up in the bottom of a pot. Another excellent material is the thin fibreglass sheeting used as a carpet underlay. I found an enormous piece of this only last week on the council dump, which will set me up for years. Ask your favourite carpet-layer to save off-cuts for you or the old pieces he takes up when laying down new.

For the drainage material itself you can use bits of broken brick and flower-pots, stones that you have raked from the garden or picked up on the beach, gravel, Vermiculite or chopped up bits of polystyrene. Pebbles and gravel are usually cheaper when bought from a builder's merchant rather than from the garden centres. The larger the container the sturdier your drainage material should be.

After this, spread a 2.5cm (1") layer of granulated sphagnum moss or pulverised bark to help conserve moisture. A layer of well-rotted and chopped up turves would be nice if you have some, but you will need to have planned this in advance. Very greedy feeders could have some well-rotted manure added at this stage or, failing that, some home-made compost. Then you are ready to add the potting compost; this can be John Innes 1, 2, or 3, the contents of last year's Gro-bag or one of the peat-based composts. Lime-haters can be given a compost free of it and alpines can have generous amounts of grit mixed into theirs. At a pinch you can, if you have a very good garden soil, use some of that, with the addition of plenty of peat and coarse sand to improve its texture.

PLANTING DETAILS

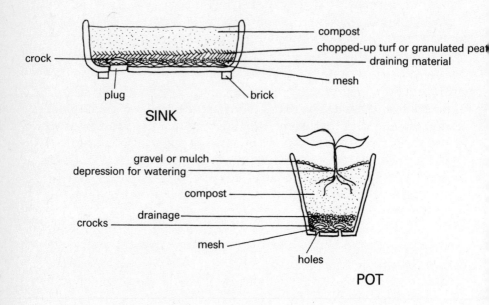

SINK

POT

You can also add your own leaf mould and compost if they are ready to use and you have enough to spare. Tired city soil will *not* do, however.

For very large containers, such as water-tanks and raised beds, it will be more economical to use bags of mixed soil, adding peat, manure, compost and leaf mould or whatever, to improve and enrich it. The better the growing medium the better the display your plants will give you, and the better their health will be. Once the containers are filled and planted up it is good to add a final top-dressing of gravel. This helps to conserve moisture, prevents soil splashing out during heavy rain or careless watering, gives the plants a cool root-run and stops the soil becoming compacted. If the containers are raised up a little, see if you can insert some kind of drip tray beneath them, as this will help to prevent staining and slippery algal growth on the paving.

As for the planting of the containers, all the methods of propagation, swapping and seeking out bargains described in Chapter 6 will apply just as much to your container plants. Almost any plant *can* be grown in a container, although some will be more successful than others, whilst the more vigorous may grow a bit too big for their boots and have to be planted out in the open garden or given away. Having said that, some thugs which would soon be out of control if planted in the open ground can be kept within bounds of a sort when container-grown. The Russian Vine is a good example of this. Left to itself in a garden it will quickly strangle everything in sight and probably lift your roof as well. One that I planted on a side wall of my house, in a moment of sheer madness, shot up two storeys in one summer, found an airbrick I did not know existed, crawled through this and suddenly appeared fountaining out of the chimney pot in the most enchanting way; but when it began to demolish the chimney, it had to be cut down and dug out. Planted in a container, on the other hand, it remains quite decorous and will twine itself prettily along a trellis or over an arbour in a biddable fashion.

It is, as always, a good idea to choose a fair proportion of the plants from those that keep their foliage throughout the year, as a collection of dead-looking twigs in bare pots will not do much to lift the spirits in the dark days. It will usually be desirable to have variations of height and shape of both plants and containers, if the scheme is not to appear monotonous, except perhaps if you have chosen a very formal plan where uniformity may be a deliberate part of the whole. For a more relaxed effect, some kind of triangular planting could be just the note, with a tree or large shrub at the back, and the other plants descending and spreading out in an irregular and slightly abandoned fashion.

Apart from the permanent planting, keep some containers to be filled with bulbs and annuals as the seasons change. If you have a quiet corner where plants can be rested when they are not doing anything special, you can ensure that those in full view are always at their peak. Remember that silver-leaved plants and white flowers can give an especially magical quality to a garden, and this effect is heightened at night. On gloomy days, the golden plants are very cheerful, so you have plenty of scope to ring the changes. If you do plan to move the plants about in this manner, you will find it helpful to have a pot trolley which you can make by screwing castors to strong pieces of timber cut to appropriate size. Onto this you can heave the pots and trundle them around quite happily. Alternatively, you can move the containers on planks, set on rollers made from lengths of strong metal piping or short scaffold poles. Tie a rope to the container and haul away, replacing the rollers as necessary.

If you have to get the containers up or down a flight of steps, place boards or an old door over the steps and fix a strong rope round the container. Then you can haul it up or lower it away. Do this with a partner, as it is easy enough to lose a finger or toe (let alone your partner) if they are trapped between the walls or the paving by a monster, completely out of control. For the sake of your back, your hernia and your relationships, keep the moving of full containers to the absolute minimum. When heavy containers *have* to be moved, try to empty them first. This is not too difficult in many cases, if you have some light plastic pots ready to comfort and protect the evicted plants. If the plants themselves are heavy, and some of those with large root-balls can be very heavy indeed, tie up their branches in plastic sheeting and place them, in their pot, onto some kind of sheet so that they can be dragged, rather than lifted to their new positions. This is also the way to deal with heavy sacks of soil and peat, etc., if you do not have a trolley or a barrow.

The after-care of plants in containers and raised beds is simple enough but essential. If you have crocked them up properly, there should be little danger of them becoming waterlogged, but they will need regular and thorough watering, as often as twice a day in hot, sunny spells, and windy conditions can also have a pronounced drying-out effect. In cool, damp, shaded conditions and during the winter months, the waterings can be reduced to once a week or even once a month, but do not rely on rain to do the job for you. It is quite difficult for sufficient rain to penetrate the foliage and soak into the compost, while plants on a sill or in the lee of a wall may be out of the reach of even the most driving rain. Peat-based composts will need even more frequent watering than other mediums. It is best to make no rash assumptions but to test the soil yourself, every day. There are various little gadgets on the market to do this, but you can make a pretty fair assessment by sticking your finger as far into the soil as possible and seeing if there is any moisture there. Lime-hating plants will prefer rainwater, and many plants will be happier with tepid water which has been standing around for a while.

Because of all this frequent watering, nutrients can be quickly leached away, so the plants will need regular feeding, about once a week in the growing season. Start feeding roughly six weeks after planting, if the plants are making some growth. Make sure they are watered before being fed, and use tepid water if possible. I prefer the liquid foods and find Phostrogen hard to beat and very economical, but I have used both Maxicrop and Tomorite with good results. A dose of sequestered iron can do wonders for a 'bad doer' and one that is showing signs of chlorosis, that is, its leaves are limp and yellowing. Read the instructions on the fertiliser very carefully and follow them exactly; overfeeding with too strong a mixture will be as bad as, if not worse than, not feeding them at all, and expensive to boot.

Plants should be re-potted every two or three years with fresh compost. If this is not possible, remove the top couple of inches from the old compost and top-dress with fresh, keeping up the liquid feeds.

All the plants will look better if you regularly remove dead leaves and dead flower heads—unless, of course, the plant bears berries or spectacular hips. The dead-heading will help to keep many plants in flower over a long period. Many shiny-leaved evergreens will enjoy having their leaves washed from time to time, to remove deposits of grime and the odd rapacious insect. Keep your eyes peeled for early warnings of attacks from pests and diseases. Prevention is better, as the saying goes, and the earlier it starts the better. Once the little brutes get established it takes a while to eliminate them, and a horrendous amount of damage can be done in a short time, which may lead to permanent injury or death, in severe cases, whilst, at the very least, the plant will be unsightly.

Container pools are fun to plant up and stock, and it can be easier to see and appreciate their inhabitants at this level. Safer, too, as it is easy enough to slide gracefully into surface-level pools when peering shortsightedly to see if the goldfish have survived the winter. They also have the great advantage of being portable. Almost all the containers and raised beds described in this chapter can be transformed into pools, by installing an inner, water-proof container, liner or a coat of rendering and sealant. The polystyrene boxes mentioned on p. 165 would be particularly good for roof-top pools. Remember, however, that if you intend to keep fish and sizeable Water-lilies in your pool, it should be not less than 45cm (18″) deep and have a surface area of 0.36 square metres (4 square feet), as described on p. 105. Any serviceable but ugly container can be prettied up with some kind of screening, such as a wall of sleepers or bricks. These can be laid dry, without nails or mortar, and can then be easily dismantled and moved if necessary. Laying the bricks in honeycomb fashion would eke them out a bit, too.

Metal containers should be given two coats of rubber or bituminous paint inside and an exterior quality top-coat, over an appropriate primer, on the outside, as I discussed on p. 166. Wooden containers can be lined with flexible plastic or PVC sheeting, stuck to the sides with rubber cement and a line of sealant run over the join. Tubs and half-casks make especially attractive pools. Sinks, of course, will need nothing more than a new plug,

although they might look better if painted black or dark brown on the inside. Bricks and blocks can either be rendered and sealed or given a liner.

If you can cultivate some air-crew, they may bring you back exotic shells, and the most desirable of these would be the handsomely ridged Giant Clam shell. This would make a beautiful miniature pool or bird-bath, or a plant container to stand beside your pool. Good shells sometimes turn up in junk shops, too.

You might consider making a raised pool against an existing wall, and this could be given a wall fountain to make it even more interesting. This could be as simple as an inverted roof or ridge tile or the afore-mentioned shell, and as elegant as a wall mask, from any of which the water can flow into the pool and from there be returned to the fountain by a submerged pump and a hidden length of pipe. Hiding the pipe *can* be a problem. You can chase it into the wall and render over it, giving the rendering a coat of paint afterwards. If the wall has a cavity, it may be possible to work the pipe up inside this. A thin skin wall of tiles or paviors can be built across the piping, or some kind of ornamental object can be propped over it, such as a fireback, a plaque, a slab of stone or a large platter. Artfully trained plants could also disguise the piping.

You can make your own masks or plaques by taking a mould from any mask or ornamental feature that you can find. Coat the original with cling-film and oil this or smear it with soft soap or Vaseline. Then press it into a container of nearly-set plaster of paris. When this has hardened completely, remove the cast and return the original to its owner. You can cast your mask in cement to which you may wish to add some colouring, or in melted down oddments of lead which you find around the place: bits of stripped-out piping and electrical conduits, or strips of flashing from a renovated roof. Your plumber may save bits for you, although you might have to give him a bob or two for them. If you have not added stainer to the cement, it can be painted afterwards either with liquid manure to tone it down or with some likely-looking colours, to resemble lead, copper, stone or terracotta.

Plant a container or raised pool in the ways described in Chapter 5, p. 107, in a layer of loam covered with gravel. Alternatively, the plants can be placed on the bottom of the pool, in perforated containers—either the purpose-made ones obtainable at water garden centres or ones that you make yourself. Holes can be drilled or burnt through any plastic pot, or you can improvise containers from chicken-wire, lined with sacking or old nylon curtains, etc., and bent up round the plants and the loam. Decrepit wicker shopping baskets will do, too.

The problem in smaller pools, as I mentioned in Chapter 5, is to keep them free of algae. The small volume of water makes them susceptible, while chemical treatments would not be safe in such a tiny area. They will need some oxygenators, but these must not be too rampant or they will choke the pool. Vallisneria would be one possibility; you might lose it in a cold winter, since it is mainly used in indoor fish-tanks and is not hardy, but you could keep some going inside the house and replant it in the tub pool in late spring, when algal growth really becomes a problem. Otherwise you can plant hardy oxygenators if you are prepared to keep thinning them out.

Lilies suitable for tubs and other small containers include *Nymphaea pygmaea* var. *alba*, 'Helvola', 'Rubra' and, in larger containers, *N.* × *laydekeri* 'Rosea', 'Lilacea', 'Purpurata' and 'Fulgens'. The floating aquatic *Hydrocharis morsus-ranae* (Frogbit) would be a good addition, too.

Remember to top the plant containers with gravel to prevent the soil clouding the water, and allow things to settle down for a few weeks before installing the fish. Instead of a fountain, you might back the wall pool with a piece of mirror, thereby appearing to double its size and lead you on into vistas beyond.

Now what about hanging baskets? you may well ask. What, indeed? To be honest, whilst I admire them greatly in municipal planting schemes, outside pubs and on the canopied decks of river steamers, I find them a perfect pain to look after myself, and this goes for wall-hung pots, too. They need watering at what feels like ten-minute intervals, and are either over-watered, in which case they will drip over all and sundry, or under-watered, whereupon all the plants will curl up and die before you can say 'Alan Titchmarsh'. You *can* line the beastly things with plastic to slow up the drying-up process, but this looks pretty horrid unless you plant through the plastic, all over the underside, to hide the stuff. You can also sink a plastic cup or yoghourt pot, which you have previously pierced all over, up to its rim in the compost at the centre of the basket. There it can be kept topped up with water and liquid feeds which will seep out through the pierced holes and keep things moist, but, Mother, is it worth it? Very occasionally, Mother answers, but only in areas so tiny that every bit of space must be utilised to the full, or in those drab spots which cannot be redeemed unless they have plants tumbling from every possible corner. So give the horrors a miss, unless, of course, you are a masochist or have far more time than is good for you, in which case you should find something better to do with it. Have you not heard of Good Works?

Finally, do please remember that any containers which are not set firmly on solid surfaces, which are, in fact, perched on balconies, sills and parapets or any other ledge, need to be secured very firmly in some way or another, whether they be cemented into place, restrained by bars, brackets and chains or simply have a couple of pieces of strong galvanised wire twisted round them and anchored to a firm surface with suitable screws or nails. These precautions are absolutely essential. It is the easiest thing in the world to dislodge them accidentally when watering or re-filling, sometimes by backing into them when stepping back to admire one's handiwork elsewhere. Anyone below who gets hit on the head by a rapidly plummeting pot of Geraniums will probably not be around long enough to sue you, but their relations will, so be warned.

9 HAUGHTYCULTURE

Roof gardens and balconies

There is something very special about roof gardening; perhaps it is the satisfaction of having wrested some beauty from these primitive surroundings. At first sight, a few bare yards of wind-lashed asphalt, cowering between the chimney pots, do not seem to promise much. But gardeners are a masochistic lot on the whole, never happier than when battling against the odds and the elements; look how we struggle to keep some tetchy little thing alive whilst we brush contemptuously past a robust beauty which is flowering its head off in a vain attempt to please.

Balconies are usually rather more congenial from the start, being, as they are, an extension of the room to which they are attached, rather than the virgin territory of a roof. Their chief drawback is the limited space which they have to offer. However, urban dwellers will wish to make the maximum use of every inch available to them. A glance round our towns and cities will show tantalising glimpses of the most ingenious roof gardens and balconies that have become veritable cornucopias, spilling out trees, shrubs, flowers, fruit and vegetables in amiable confusion. Take a camera, sketch-book and note-pad with you on your travels to record such felicities, so that they may inspire and spur you on to achieve your own Babylonian triumphs.

The basic principles are the same for both areas. It will be essential to find out if the existing structures are sound and strong enough to take the weight of whatever you plan to install thereon . . . Do not be tempted to take chances over this, but get professional advice from an architect, surveyor or competent builder. No matter how light your compost and your container may be initially, once the compost is wet it can become very heavy indeed. Remember that 4.5 litres (1 gallon) of water weigh about 4.5kg (10lbs), and that a container large enough to take a small tree or a large shrub may take at least 9 litres (2 gallons) of water a day, so you can see how quickly the weight can mount up.

If you move into your house when it is being ripped apart or renovated, it will not be too difficult to have the roof strengthened at this stage. Later on there are still ways of beefing things up a bit, but this is not for the amateur. However, remember that the roof will be strongest at its edges and over any joists, so concentrate your planting, etc., there. Spreading the load helps a bit, too, so some form of decking would be effective, either over the entire roof or under groups of containers.

The surface of the roof is important. If it is concrete or tiled, you are in luck as it will take a lot of traffic and provide a good surface for whatever you put up there, but frequently the flat roof is lead, or asphalt, and this is often scattered with gravel chippings which look sturdy enough, like a gravel path, but in hot weather, when the asphalt softens, any sharp or weighty object placed on it, or heavy traffic across it, will push the gravel down through the asphalt making holes which will leak, causing endless problems with damp. Unless you can remove the gravel and tile the roof instead, it would be wise to cover the whole area with decking which you can make simply enough from skip timber or wooden battens, which will have to be treated with a preservative. This is not too expensive a solution and it has the advantage that you can make the decks at various levels to give more interest to what is usually rather a boring flatness.

A roof is one of the few places in which I would consider using Astro-turf. Because a sky-high garden is, in itself, an artificial conceit, such outright imitation is acceptable, I think. It is also a remarkably comfortable solution to the extremes of hot and cold found in such situations. On sunny days, the roof can become unbearably hot, whilst in damp or icy weather, it can be chill or dangerously slippery. Astro-turf insulates you from either of these excesses, is very easy to maintain and pleasant to the touch, ideal for sunbathers, in fact. However, it is hardly within the reach of the poor but honest gardener, so you will have to search out second-hand bargains or off-cuts, from shops and exhibitions. For a very small area, you might be able to lash out on a few yards and economise on something else.

If your roof is strong enough and you are prepared for hours of maintenance, there is nothing to stop you having a real lawn up there, but I advise against it. The turf, being of necessity on a thin layer of soil, will dry out at an alarming rate in fine weather, and the thought of trotting up and down with a lawn mower amongst the over-amorous pigeons is distinctly unnerving.

Whatever surface you choose, it is essential to make efficient provision for drainage. Of necessity, the roof will already have, one hopes, its own adequate drainage system, so your main concern will be not to obstruct, overload or choke this in any way. It is a good idea to fit some kind of protection, such as a sediment trap, or a cover of perforated zinc or crumpled chicken-wire, over all drainage outlets, so that they do not become clogged by dead leaves and other garden gunge. It is also worth installing something which will help to prevent the compost from being washed out of the containers on the roof, for not only would the seepage cause staining of the roof surfaces but it could lead to the formation of mosses and algal growth which would make the roof a dangerous place for the unwary.

The subject of drains leads me to the water supply. I know that it should, logically, be the other way round, but there it is, that's the way my mind works—backwards. On the roof, above all, install an outdoor tap and a wall-mounted hose, if you are contemplating anything more than one geranium and a pot of Basil. The initial outlay will be amply repaid by the survival rate of the plants. Good intentions are one thing, but actions are another. At the end of a long, hot and tiring day, even the most dedicated may flop guiltily into the nearest chair rather than face the prospect of trailing round the roof with can after can of water. If you absolutely cannot afford an outside tap, fix up a primitive irrigation system by perforating an old length of hose which can be connected easily to the nearest tap. It will lead, inevitably, to a messy puddle at the tap end, for I have yet to find a really waterproof connection, but your plants may survive.

Should the roof be up to it, a water-butt or cistern would be a help. It could be filled by the winter rains and topped up by an occasional session with the hose. It might even be possible to channel water from surrounding roofs into your personal reservoir. A barrel would be pleasant-looking, but an old water tank of

galvanised metal or plastic would be quite serviceable, and the latter could be given a 'hide'. From these tanks you can fill your cans in a comparatively painless fashion and the plants will appreciate the tepid water much more than they would a cold douche. You will often find water tanks on skips and your plumber would probably be able to obtain one for you. Failing this, any watertight container, the larger the better, that you can get up on to the roof will do.

Talking of which, if access to your lofty plot is limited, it is usually possible to fix up a Jenny-wheel, which is a sort of rope and pulley on a scaffolding-pole, with which you can haul up all that you need. These can be hired quite easily and cheaply, or a friendly builder might lend you one. Really ambitious roof-gardeners have hired cranes to swing a container-load of mature trees and exotic 'features' up on to their eyries, but I cannot pretend that this is an economical proposition unless you are on extremely intimate terms with the crane-driver.

But back to the water tank. Give the more homely fellows a disguise of some kind; perhaps a screen of light timber with a generously proportioned evergreen plant strategically placed before it. *Anything* you can do to make watering easy and enjoyable will be time and money well spent. All container-grown plants need full and regular watering, but those on a roof will need even more attention as they are particularly exposed to both sun and wind which can be equally desiccating, a point which is often overlooked.

Lighting is an important addition to roof life; it will both prolong and enhance the time you spend up there and be an additional safety factor. Any electrical fittings will need to be installed by a competent electrician, using special cables and connections. One or two spot-lights, whether uppers or downers, will have the most dramatic effect. However, all sorts of oil lamps and candle lanterns can provide perfectly adequate and absolutely charming effects. A string of candle lanterns, strung across the roof above the heads of its inhabitants, and some artfully placed jam-jars containing night-lights or more candles, can all be used to add some mystery and magic.

At chimney-level, the wind does not just dry out the containers rapidly, it can scorch, break or even uproot your plants as well as bringing *you* out in goose-bumps, so that all the protection that you can devise will be a necessity and a boon. For the welfare of the plants, a perforated screen can be as good as, if not better than, a solid barrier. These can be as strong as a honeycomb wall, a slatted fence or stout trellis; as ingenious as a rope threaded between two horizontal bars or bamboo canes lashed to supporting timbers, whilst more flimsy solutions include split-cane screening, expanding trellis panels and various kinds of wire and plastic meshing. These last will have to be covered pretty thoroughly with climbers to make them acceptable. Strong or flimsy, they will need a secure framework and firm fixing if they are not to be torn free of their moorings by the frolicsome winds which can reach gale force from time to time.

Unlike the plants, we humans will prefer something more solid between us and the prevailing winds, on at least part of the roof. This may be found in the lee of a chimney stack or neighbouring walls, but if it does not exist, we will want to provide such a sheltered area. Here again there are many possibilities. There are expensive glass panels and slightly cheaper ones of rigid plastic; these you might copy for yourself. A small wall might be built against the winds if the strength of the roof would allow it, to shelter a table and some chairs. The whole garden could be enclosed with fencing panels or just a corner of it, to protect a sunbather, perhaps. It would be quite possible to build your own wall or fencing from skip timber, but you must remember that an Englishman's home is no longer his (or her) castle. We are beset with restrictions and regulations on all sides. You will have to check with your local planning department and the building inspector before you do anything on a roof, unless you are the lucky possessor of some hidden gullies, in which case you might get away with a trick or two. Your landlord or freeholder may also have placed some dastardly restrictions in your lease, whilst even your neighbours may be able to scupper your plans, so proceed with care.

At very least, you should be able to make yourself some temporary screening. An old screen could be used, recovered with canvas, maybe, or a clothes-horse, similarly covered. A little group of these could help. You could nail a light trellis to a wooden frame and hinge two or three of these panels together. Backed with canvas or hessian, they would be effective and easily stowed away, and just as easily put up, to be moved around the roof to follow the sun, dodge the wind and foil any neighbours who might be goggling at your antics. You could consider giving your screens an inner lining of foil-covered hardboard to double up the dose of sun, thus turning you to a very fetching shade if you are lucky, or, alas, a rather repellant one if you are like me. The larger sizes of kitchen foil could be used, or the linings of tea chests, if you should come across one. Failing these, you can buy from your local glass cutters some adhesive-backed mirror foil which they use to back looking-glass destined for exterior work.

With all these essentials dealt with, you can concentrate on the trimmings. Walls can be trellised or painted in jolly or sophisticated colours, while those of you handy with a brush can let your fancy rip. You could turn a chimney stack into a Gothick folly or a ruined Doric column; paint a romantic landscape, a luscious jungle or, if you are not so talented, you could surely manage a naïve simplicity. Even the most cack-handed could probably draw and paint a couple of lollypop trees in tubs, an unashamedly-unlikely flower and a smiling sun in a blue sky, which could cheer things up no end.

The smallest roof or balcony can be apparently doubled in size by a mirror or two, artfully placed and disguised. Bits of mirror can still be picked up quite easily and not too expensively in all the usual haunts. Quite small pieces can be fitted like panes into a false door or window frame, which would appear to open on to yet another garden beyond, whilst larger pieces, from wardrobe doors or stripped-out bathrooms, shops and restaurants, can be used to back an archway or a wrought-iron gate. The glazier will cut them to shape if you wish, but you could just cut out your arch from plywood off-cuts and fit these over the glass, along with any 'glazing bars' of wooden moulding stuck on with Araldite. Alternatively, you can paint your arch, door, window, grille or whatever directly on to the glass. As always, the mirrors must be set at a very slight angle so that they reflect, not the onlooker but another part of the roof garden or *another* mirror, in which case, the illusion of space will be, appropriately enough, limitless. The glass should be backed with the foil I mentioned previously and then should be stuck to a piece of plywood with a suitable glue which your glazier will supply. It is a good idea to run round the bare edges of glass with that bath sealant which comes in a plastic tube. Any form of coping, porch or pediment will help to protect the glass. I know that the whole idea seems a bit twee, but when well done it can look marvellous, and the artifice is acceptable on the roof.

Water is just as desirable on a roof as elsewhere in a garden. Bearing in mind its weight, position it carefully, deciding as usual between still water with fish and plants, or moving water, whether a small jet fountain or something bubbling and trickling gently. With a jet fountain, remember that the winds up on the roof are capable of carrying the plume of water over a considerable area, which could cause annoyance to your neighbours or actual damage to their property, so make sure that any jet of water is small enough to be contained within your boundaries, no matter how sportive the wind. The same care will have to be exercised when watering the garden by hose or sprinkler. As the roof is strongest at its edges, it may well be that a wall fountain will be the answer for you, but your roof pool can be made in most of the ways described in Chapter 5 and in most of the containers mentioned in Chapter 8, choosing the lightest ones whenever possible, unless you have a very strong roof.

Because extreme heat can be as much a problem as the wind, some kind of shade would be a welcome addition to the amenities.

A cheap beach umbrella will do well enough, if you stick to the plainest colours or stripes, rather than some overblown floral print which will make you feel dizzy—the last thing you want in this airy oasis. Sun blinds of canvas or split-cane can also be used, propped up and out on some upright posts. A simple pergola of skip timber would be easy enough to make, and if you are *really* hopeless at carpentry, unable to screw or nail two bits of wood together, there are some useful little metal joints that you can buy, made by the same people who make metal fence posts. Into these, you can just push the ends of the timber. The joints come in various kinds so that you should be able to find some to suit your design. Measure up carefully and cut your timber (or get the timber merchant to do it for you, if you are buying new wood) in appropriate lengths; what could be simpler? If there is no suitable surface on which to secure the uprights, treat the bottom of the posts with an extra coat or two of preservative and sink each post into a container of soil, into which you can also pop a climber which will grow up and round the post, and over the pergola in a thoroughly satisfactory manner.

Alternatively, you could fix two horizontal bars between adjoining walls or chimney stacks; to these you fix cross-bars of timber, thus forming your pergola, which is an even easier solution. If high-tech is your sort of thing, you could use lengths of scaffold poles or old iron piping to form your uprights, to which you would fix lengths of planking, more piping or rope.

All space on a roof is precious and every inch of wall should be used. Nothing softens the harsh outlines of modern or urban architecture more charmingly than a riot of social climbers, ruthlessly ascending by every toe and finger hold; or, as is the way of such creatures, tumbling down again, covered in confusion and a blush of blossom. What goes up must come down, somebody, probably Nanny, once said. And very useful this is for the speedy coverage of every unappealing surface. Practically anything that climbs will dangle just as happily so that, by the neat arrangement of a series of containers at different heights, your camouflage will be accomplished in double-quick time. These combinations of

screening and planting can be used just as effectively to hide an eyesore or to frame a delightful prospect. Make gaps or windows in the screen or green wall to provide a peep-hole to the outer world if there is a sight to be seen. If not, make your barrier a total one and enjoy your secret garden in solipsistical splendour.

As for the plants and their containers, the choice is not nearly so narrow as you might think, given the exposed site. All the containers mentioned in Chapter 8 will do, depending on the strength of the roof, but for your own well-being, the lighter they are the better and the less risk you take of back-strain and hernia, when lugging them about. For the heavier containers, remember to spread the load and give them a small deck of their own if the roof is not already covered in this fashion. If the roof is strong enough to take a raised bed you are in luck, for most plants will be happier with their roots less confined and the compost will not dry out so quickly, especially if you line the beds with plastic sheeting or a coat of bituminous paint. All the usual methods of making a raised bed can be used, but remember that if one side of the bed is against an existing structural wall, you must install a serious vertical damp-proof course if you are not to cause real problems. Take expert advice, but in many cases you can give the wall two or three coats of an exterior wall-proofing substance such as Aquaseal or Synthaproof and then line the bed with plastic sheeting. This should do the trick, but it is worth making sure by checking with your builder.

Lightweight but primitive beds can be made quite cheaply by using chicken-wire, strengthened in some way by timber battens or strong galvanised wire and angle-iron, perhaps, which you then line with plastic and fill with compost and drainage material in the usual way. These can then be disguised by some lightweight 'hide', such as skip timber trellis, or a roll of half logs which you can buy at garden centres, etc., or by planting directly through the mesh and plastic with trailing and mat-forming plants, so that the unlovely outlines of the bed are hidden. Ivy of course, Vinca, *Cerastium tomentosum*, Aubrieta, Alyssum and all the other bushy, spreading little plants would do the trick. The effect should be something like a natural mound rather than a bed, and would fit quite well into an informal scheme. If your roof is concrete, you could consider covering it with gravel which would complete the rustic effect, but you would have to fit some metal gauze over the drain-traps and down-pipes to prevent the gravel being washed into them.

A bed of peat blocks is another possible solution for a raised bed. The blocks are light to handle when dry, but once they are on the roof they must be soaked before use. They can be laid like bricks or stone, and the walls should slope slightly backwards with soil sprinkled between each layer and plants inserted as you build. Their roots will grow into the blocks and help to bind the wall. You will have to keep the bed well watered as the blocks would shrink and eventually crumble if allowed to dry out. One way to prevent this would be to provide the bed with a length of perforated hosepipe which you could easily connect to a tap and so keep them gently irrigated.

Whatever kind of raised bed you decide upon, they will all need a good layer of drainage material at the bottom and some weep-holes as well, although these will not be necessary for a bed made of peat blocks. Weep-holes are placed at the bottom of the retaining walls to allow surplus water to drain away. This is particularly necessary in the wet, windy months, when the plants could drown if not given effective drainage. Another idea is to place lengths of plastic piping at the bottom of the beds. These should be perforated at the top and sides to allow the water to enter the pipes and to be carried out through the sides of the bed at a point which will drain to the nearest outlet or down-pipe. These pipes should be covered by a good layer of drainage material which can be crocks, bits of old bricks, stones, pebbles, gravel or fired-clay granules, such as Hortag. Even broken-up bits of polystyrene foam can be used and these would be especially light. Odd lengths of plastic piping are often found on skips and so are broken bricks and other rubble, so you should be able to do all this cheaply enough. For an added precaution, I would place a small piece of metal or nylon gauze over the inside of the weep-holes and indeed over the drainage holes of any roof-top containers, as the less gunge that escapes the better. You could also use the thin fibreglass carpet-underlay that I mentioned earlier for this purpose.

It is amazing how many plants will thrive on a roof-garden if you site them sensibly and give them a little care and attention. The outer ring of planting will have to be able to stand up to the wind and many of our native plants will do this. However, *leylandii* is a good tough evergreen plant, and makes a solid barrier. *Thuja occidentalis* and its cultivars are also good. As I said in Chapter 6, these conifers are best planted when small, before their roots have been constricted by a container. Hollies, Cotoneasters, *Viburnum tinus*, the taller Euonymus, Yew and Pittosporums are all tolerant of the winds and, although Privet is not always regarded as being especially wind resistant, I have used it on some very exposed roofs with good results. Tough climbers include the Ivies, *Clematis montana* and its varieties, Honeysuckles, *Jasminum officinale*, the dreaded Russian Vine and the delicate looking Passion Flower.

Within these outer windbreaks, a vast range of plants will thrive, and many will particularly enjoy the good drainage that raised beds and containers provide. You will be able to find plants for both shaded and sunny positions, as well as those that will be happy in either. I have grown the Eucalypts, Fatsias, Mahonias, Ligustrums, Choisyas, Yuccas, Cordylines, Skimmias, Roses, Rhododendrons, Hebes, Hydrangeas, a variety of silver darlings and a host of others, as well as fruit, vegetables, herbs, bulbs and bedding plants of all kinds. Many fruit and vegetables are as charming as they are useful, whilst the herbs are both, and fragrant to boot. Potatoes, Strawberries, Alpine Strawberries and many herbs, especially Parsley and the Thymes, can be grown in barrels of wood, plastic or clay, which have had planting holes provided all over their sides. These days, you can buy fruit-trees grown on dwarfing-rootstocks, and these are the ones to go for. It is even possible to buy trees where two or three varieties have been grafted on to a single trunk. Tomatoes do well on a roof and are easily grown in Gro-bags. Last year's Gro-bags can be used for filling a container the following year.

You will have to choose your compost according to your plants. While the peat-based composts are light to handle and excellent for many plants, they do not have much holding power for large plants, which need something a bit more solid to help them withstand the winds. Whatever container and soil you choose, try to fit some kind of drip tray underneath the container, as this will help to prevent the roof becoming stained and slippy, which can easily happen as a result of the constant watering and feeding that the plants will need.

If you feel that all this will leave little room for your private life, you will have to go all out for a garden of total or near total artifice: it must be trellis, paintwork, furniture and ornament, with perhaps one really striking plant and a pot of herbs or annuals which you should just about manage to keep fed and watered. With a floor of decking, tiles or Astro-turf, brightly painted walls adorned by a mural or panels of trellis, a table, some chairs and perhaps an urn or *objet trouvé*, you could have most of the pleasure with none of the pain, a thoroughly immoral but always pleasurable thought. Without the help of plants, you would have to have panels of slats or trellis to disguise drain-pipes and other hideous horrors.

If, however, you do decide to go for the full treatment, plants and all, you will need to find somewhere to keep tools, the hose and fertilisers, etc.—all the impediments of gardening life, from plant ties to spray guns, by way of hoof and horn, in fact. It may be that you will have room for a cupboard near the garden door, but most of us will have to find somewhere on the roof itself. The hose can be coiled up at the bottom of a container, which can then have another, shallower container, that will just fit inside its rim, placed over the top. Bags of fertiliser can also be stored in this way, but they will need to be placed inside well-fastened plastic bags to protect them from drips from the pot above. The plants in the top

STORAGE

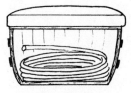

Cushion seat on
half-barrel to
hide a hose

Plant pot with
hand tools and
plant food, etc.

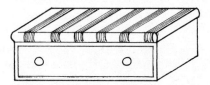

A box seat and cushion made
from an old drawer, to store
large tools, etc.

Hollow brick box in which to
hide tools, etc., topped with
slab or wood to make a table

container can trail gracefully or nod away, while the contents below will remain well-hidden.

Another idea is to make a box seat to keep all the equipment in. This can be given either a fitted cushion or a pile of loose ones to make it a pleasant place to sit, or it could be used plain as a small table to hold drinks, magazines, etc. The simplest way to make this seat, if you do not have any wooden chests already, is to find a large drawer from a piece of damaged junk furniture; a chest of drawers or wardrobe, perhaps. Use the smallest drawers for containers, and the largest for your seats and tables. The lid can be any strong and waterproof material that you can find. A couple of paving slabs would do, but choose light ones. Timber of any kind, even chipboard, if covered with tiling set in a waterproof cement and given a waterproof grout. Another way to waterproof interior quality materials is to nail, staple or stud some plastic-coated material over them. These can be had in strong, plain colours or various patterns. If you cannot find or make such a wooden seat, make one of a few bricks or blocks, and give them a similar lid. This way you could keep even quite large tools safe and hidden, but I would give them all a wipe with an oily rag to prevent rust, or a quick burst from an aerosol of lubricant for the same purpose. Even a dustbin could do the job effectively, lightly and neatly. You could screen it with some trellis or an evergreen plant. If the tools, fertilisers, hose and 'medicine chest' are up there and easy to get at, there is far more chance that your high-flying pets will survive.

It may well be that your efforts will spur on your neighbours to colonise their roofs, too, and that you will be surrounded by charming vistas as far as the eye can see. If, however, this does not happen and all about you is drear brickwork, try an old trick; press wall flower seeds and the like into little balls of compost and squidgy clay, then hurl these, with as much force as you can muster, at every neighbouring wall. Some of them should be on target and stay put. With luck the seeds will germinate and put out roots into the mortar. In theory, you could be surrounded by fountains of flowers next spring. Well, it is *only* a suggestion, you do not have to carry it out, but look how it would amuse the sparrows.

10 HIDDEN DEPTHS

Basements and courtyards

Here we go, if not from the sublime to the ridiculous, at least *de haut en bas*, as it were. When you see an estate agent's particulars commending a charming garden flat with own patio, you can be sure it is a damp basement with a dreary, concrete-screeded well, containing some dead leaves and an old Coke tin. If they offer you an *exceptional* garden flat, with own delightfully landscaped garden, it will be much the same, but with a second damp bedroom and a larger yard which will have had eight concrete slabs laid over the existing screed, and there will be a dead bay tree in a wooden tub at the far corner. But do not be dispirited. I cannot promise to cure the internal damp (and nor can anyone else, I fear, from long experience), but we can cheer up the 'patio' no end. It is true that you are likely to have almost permanent shade in all or the greater part of the area, but several of the most engaging plants prefer it this way, so why should you complain?

I would begin the transformation with the walls; there is a movement in chic circles to decry white-painted walls; 'Who would want to live in a white shoe-box?' they ask in a scornful manner. Well, I would, for one; if I have to live in a shoe-box, you can bet your life it will be a white one, the whiter the better; although I might make brief forays and experiments with acid yellow and warm terracotta in the odd corner or alcove, to set off a particular plant. But white will do very nicely indeed, and by the time you have painted every bit of wall and every beastly bit of pipe-work dazzling white, you will begin to feel better. Of course, if you feel like painting one of the murals I have described previously, or installing a bit of deceitful mirror-work, and some *trompe l'oeil* trellising, you will be in danger of fulfilling the agent's descriptions. The down pipes can be cheered up even further by planting a climber, or painting Jack's beanstalk to sprawl up and over them.

With the walls attended to, you could treat the floor as your next priority. Whenever possible, retain or obtain some areas of earth, even if you have to break up a bit of concrete to get to it. Do not worry if this leaves some jagged edges as these can be disguised by a brick or timber edging of some kind. Plants that you wish to grow vigorously enough to cover a large area of wall or trellis are far more likely to reach for the sky if their roots can go deep into the earth, even starved city dirt. You can excavate some of this sad stuff and replace it or enrich it with something a little more gastronomic to nurture the climbers. If the floor has been tiled or slabbed too well for you to risk disturbing it, or if the prospect fills you with alarm, you will have to find a largish container if your plants are to get away satisfactorily. This is where the raised beds and the old water cisterns come into their own.

But back to the floor. Gravel goes down very well over concrete, so long as you remember those drain covers. Decking is another pleasant solution and so is Astro-turf, as this is one more area where it is permissible. You could lay some bricks, tiles or slabs, if you find a cheap supply, but you must be careful to lay them below the airbricks and the damp-proof course. You can make your own slabs, of course, quite simply, by making some hinged wooden moulds, either square, oblong or in assorted sizes, from odds and ends of rescued wood. The slabs could be of any dimension that you choose, but smaller ones will be lighter to handle, of course. Slabs of 30cm or 45cm (12″ or 18″) are quite manageable. Lay a sheet of polythene on a level surface and place the hinged timber frame on this. Make up a strong, stiff sand-and-cement or concrete mixture. You can colour the mixture if you wish, but do be restrained about this and, for goodness sake, do not have a bilious mixture of red and yellow slabs, or your hangovers will be even worse than usual. Pour some of the concrete mixture into the mould and pull a piece of straight timber across the top to level it off. Unhinge the frame carefully and move it a few centimetres away, still on the polythene sheeting, before repeating the process. Obviously, you will need a bit of space for this, as the slabs will have to be left where they are until they have 'gone off'. These home-made slabs can also be joined together with a little more sand-and-cement to make containers and the sides of raised beds, which can then be painted white to match the walls.

Another way to pave the floor would be to make a grid of timber battens or bricks over the base and pour the concrete into the grid. The bricks or timber would stay in position and could look rather smart, but you would have to treat the wood with a suitable preservative. Your builder's merchant would advise you on the correct mixes for your purposes. Alternatively, if the existing screed is in good order, you could consider painting it (there are special paints for this) either a plain colour to match or contrast with the rest of your scheme, or draw out a squared pattern on the floor and paint alternate squares in chess-board fashion. Black and white would be quite dashing.

If you enjoy playing about with cement in this fashion, you could try making some concrete boxes or imitation sinks. This can be done in the same way as that I described for making a concrete plinth in Chapter 7: cover a wooden box, which you have found or made, with chicken-wire, by stapling it on. Then brush or trowel on a stiff sand-and-cement mixture or the hypertufa mixture used to cover china sinks. Rough the drying surface up a bit with your finger-tips and then stain with liquid manure or paint it, when it is quite dry. The one advantage a basement has over a roof is that you need not worry about weight, so that you can make your beds and containers as large and heavy as you like, so long as you leave a little space between them in which to move about, but remember to install that vertical d.p.c. between the soil and the house walls if you are making the beds there. I am sorry to keep banging on about this, but you do not want any *more* problems in your troglodyte's lair, do you?

There are sure to be some man-holes just where they are most

HOMEMADE CONCRETE PAVING

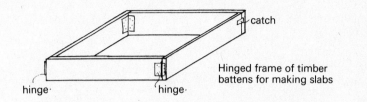

catch

Hinged frame of timber
battens for making slabs

hinge·   hinge·

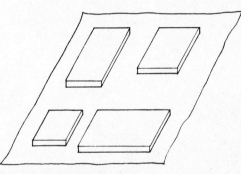

Assorted homemade concrete
slabs drying on a polythene
sheet

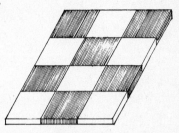

Black and white slabs

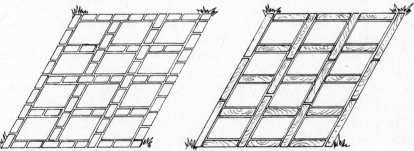

Concrete poured between
bricks or wooden battens

inconvenient, and you will have to disguise them as best you may, either by fitting them with a recessed cover into which you can fit whatever you are using to cover the rest of the area, or by painting them to match, if they are sitting where you cannot mask them with a slab, or a plant in a container.

The gloomier the basement, the more light you will want to introduce. You have made a good start by painting the walls and brightening the floor. A piece of mirror-glass will reflect and make the most of any light there is. At this level, it can be a false door, window, or arch, in the way I have suggested for roof gardens. It can also be the centre-piece to an arched panel of trellis which might have a planted urn on a pedestal placed in front of it. You would get double the light and double the plant this way. Artificial lighting will help, of course, at night, or on particularly gloomy days. If you cannot afford electrical fittings, go for all the oil lamps and candles that you can fit in. I had a really dark basement flat in South Kensington; no one could have called it a garden flat, but it had three gloomy wells. With a lot of white paint, green plants, and those obliging annuals that flower in the shade, plus all the lights I could find, they became pleasant places in which to sit and eat. At night, they were extra-special with the lights playing on the large leaves of the Fatsias and the fretted leaves of the little Japanese Maples. If the night is a fine one, you can bring out lamps from the house on extension leads, for a special occasion, so long as there is no wetness about.

When it comes to planting out in the basement, there are two basic approaches and many options between the two. The first is to rely on just one or two really striking plants, suitably framed by a false arch or trellis, either constructed from salvaged materials or painted directly onto the wall. Years ago, I found a Victorian marble statue of a nymph, in the shabby (in those days) jumble of shops in Westbourne Grove. It cost thirty pounds, which was a fortune to me then, but we have been together now for thirty years, except for a brief period when she was stolen and recovered six months later from a shop in the Kings Road. I gave her pride of place in one of those South Kensington basements, with just a pair of pots, planted with a pyramid of Ivy, on each side of her. She looked wonderful and needed nothing else to set off her charms. Failing a nymph, make yourself an obelisk of painted timber or trellis, find a particularly impressive chimney pot, or *paint* one of these straight on to the wall. Put a standard tree on each side, or a cone of clipped ivy, and you will have much the same effect. You can dream up your own variations on these themes.

The opposite school of thought believes in throwing in as many plants as can be assembled and letting them get on with it, more or

MIRRORS

Trellised arch
backed with mirror

False window and Gothic ply
over mirror glass

False arch of half-bricks
backed with mirror

False door with mirror panes

Mirror-backed gate

less. This is much the effect that I lean to, preferring things to be in a state of barely controlled chaos, which is just as well, as that is how most of my gardens end up, with the controlled bit becoming less and less apparent. If you give the plants a reasonable amount and quality of soil, they will do you proud, even in the shadiest of places. Several roses will flower bravely with never a glimpse of the sun. 'Mermaid' grows well in the shade and 'New Dawn', 'Madame Alfred Carrière' and 'Danse du Feu' are amongst those that will put up a good struggle against all odds. I have never seen 'Bantry Bay' recommended for shade, but I have two, each in a 45cm (18") pot, by a north-facing doorway, which flower their heads off all summer long. The Japanese Maples and the Rhododendron family, which includes the Azaleas, are all happiest in light shade. Fatsias, Choisyas, Aucubas, Skimmias, *Viburnum tinus* and the Fuchsias, all grow well in shade or dappled shade, as do a great many others.

In fact a number of plants, which you will see described as needing to be grown on a south-facing wall, will do amazingly well on a shaded north wall. *Clematis armandii* and *Actinidia kolomitka* have done splendidly for me in deep shade, as well as those things which are *supposed* to like it: the climbing Hydrangea, Winter Jasmine and all sorts of Ivies, for instance, plus many Clematis. Because space in a basement is limited, I would even allow my *bêtes noires*, the hanging and wall baskets, a place here. In the shade, they will not dry out at such a ridiculous speed as they do elsewhere. Old wicker bicycle baskets, lined with plastic, make good wall containers and you will be able to think of others. Ivies will grow happily in them, and so will Busy Lizzies, Tobacco plants and fibrous-rooted Begonias in the summer, while in the winter you could try small Aucubas, winter-flowing Pansies, and perhaps some Primulas.

It might be a waste to buy special furniture for such a small area, for you can always move the indoor furniture out quite easily, but old kitchen chairs and tables would look right, painted to match your other paintwork, or stripped and sealed. You could make a simple table, and benches to match, of slatted timber, or cover any old junk table with a cloth of some kind to pretty it up. If there is a flight of stairs down to your basement, your garden tools could be under them, or you could keep them in a box seat or cushion-topped container, as I suggested in the last chapter. Granular and liquid fertilisers will obviously take less room than sacks of manure, and be less obtrusive in every way.

A pool will be a charming addition to any basement. Because of the limited space, a wall pool would be ideal. Without much light, Water-lilies would be unlikely to flower, but various foliage plants would be happy enough, and you could place container-grown plants around the pool so that they could lean over to admire their reflections in the still water. A wall fountain would make things even more entrancing, as just the sound of flowing water is greatly soothing, unless, of course, you have a weak bladder.

You may wish to 'roof-in' part or whole of your basement, to make a green room and drat the sunlight. It should be simplicity itself to place some timber beams across the area and grow climbers over these, which should be conducive to many a green thought in a green shade. More elaborate, arched roofs can be made by bending slender slats over to a central beam, or by cutting half-hoops from plywood and nailing straight slats up and round these. Simplest of all could be to place a couple of panels of trellis across the area, supported on horizontal bearers, screwed to the walls. Panels of glass or clear plastic fitted at a gentle slope over a part of this roofing would give added protection, and it would be charming to sit out there as the rain pattered down overhead.

If you have young children and the basement is their only play area, you would do well, for the sake of your sanity, to rig it out for their exclusive use. String a strong beam across the area, and from this hang old tyres, a home-made swing, trapeze, rope-ladder, climbing rope and rings. They are all easily made from oddments of timber and rope and, depending on the size of the beam, can be hung up in groups or in succession, onto strong hooks. The floor could be painted into a hopscotch grid and some kind of climbing-

frame-cum-play-house could be placed in a corner. If there is no room for the climbing frame, you could certainly make a wig-wam of bamboo and remnants. Any largish circular container could have its base removed and be screwed high up on a wall to make a net-ball goal. A bit of netting could be strung across the area to provide a net for 'Badminton', whilst you could make some easily removed protection to slip over the windows so that the children could hit a ball about with a tennis racquet. It might not be the most beautiful area in the world, but at least you should be on speaking terms with your children at the end of the day. The smallest could have a sandpit, paddling pool and tray for water play, all of which would take up very little space, but give an enormous amount of joy, for a minimum outlay, and your interiors would be spared.

If you 'rescue' all the materials and propagate all the plants, you can, within a season, transform these unprepossessing dungeons into the most engaging bowers, using annual climbers and bedding plants grown from seed, to make a quick showing whilst the permanent plants get their act together over the months. Now that I am living in a house without a basement, I rather envy you the fun you can have and the dramatic effects you can contrive so economically and so easily. You will still have to feed, water and dead-head, of course, but the watering in shaded basements is a far less onerous task than it is anywhere else, as the containers will dry out more slowly and they are all so close to hand that it is a positive pleasure to potter about with a watering can and a multi-purpose spray. In a few minutes the chores will be ended and you can sink back, sip a little dry white wine and reach for your copy of *The Great Gardens of Britain*.

11   CARE AND CONTROL ORDERS

Aftercare and maintenance

The school in the Hampshire village where I lived for a while had a notice which impressed me. It read *'Church of England Mixed Infants (Controlled)'*. I wondered how they managed it. My mixed infants were anything but controlled, and the same went for my garden, where the little darlings, over whom, in theory, I kept a firm hand, romped and rioted despite me, attacking each other without provocation. The bullies of the plant world elbowed everything else out of the way, while the wimps sat wilting and whingeing in odd corners. It does not pay to let your garden get the upper hand. Plants are expensive in time and money; it makes no sense to let them do each other in. It is a good idea to make regular, un-announced tours of inspection round the garden, and nip any signs of insurrection in the bud, as it were. Take a pair of sharp scissors or secateurs with you, and a small roll of garden wire or some plant ties. This way, you can nip off dead flowerheads and any bits of the plants that are diseased, prune back or cut out any superfluous growth, and pinch out growing shoots to encourage the lean and lanky to bush out and thicken up a bit. Stragglers and bullies can be restrained and retrained, while degenerate floppers can be given the cane—bamboo, that is.

Of course, it all starts way back, at the preparatory stages. If you prepared the ground properly and planted sensibly, you will have given your plants the best of starts, but that does not mean that you can sit back and let nature get on with things, my goodness, no. As you will probably have gathered by now, a garden is not made by sitting in the shade and saying, 'Oh how beautiful, how beautiful'; which is a perfectly revolting phrase that my father used to hurl at us when we were slacking at the weeding. It's a wonder that we remained fond of gardening, but we did.

You will have to keep up with the watering above all, even in the most labour-saving of gardens. Except for those plants that like a poor soil, which are usually the silver-leaved things of Mediterranean origin, the ground will need to be kept fed and fertile, while all new plants will have to be given a chance to develop, which will mean keeping them free from weeds until they are strong enough to smother the competition. Anything tall and slender should be provided with a stake or a cane if it is not to be rocked and broken by the wind or careless passers-by, whether they be two- or four-footed. Fruit trees and bushes will all require some protection from the birds, and almost every plant in the garden will need some kind of spray at one time or other, although the healthier the plant, the less medication it should require. It would be well worth trying out some preventative medicine, too. Even if it did not work it would be unlikely to do harm; which is more than you can say for most commercial products, although I do use these when desperate, from time to time.

There is a splendid little book called *Companion Plants* by Helen Philbrick and Richard B. Gregg which will give you a lot of good ideas on this subject, but the following general hints are worth trying. Garlic should be planted near each Rose plant, as this does help to keep them free of greenfly; ground infested with couch grass is said to be cleared if planted thickly with Tomato plants or Turnip seeds, while the beastly little French and African Marigolds are meant to be beneficial to practically everything, killing nematodes (eelworms) in the soil and frightening off whitefly, amongst other virtues; *Tagetes minuta*, the Mexican Marigold, is supposed to overcome ground elder and marestail. All members of the Onion family help to keep Carrots free from carrot fly, and Nasturtiums, grown at the base of, and up, an apple tree will repel Woolly Aphis. The Mint family is beneficial to the Brassicas, as their pungent smell repels many pests. I would not recommend planting Mint directly into the soil amongst the Cabbages, but pot it up in old buckets or similar containers and sink these into the ground, with about 15cm (6″) of the container above the surface, so that the Mint is kept within bounds. You will have to keep an eye on it, even so, or it will overflow its bin and root all around. Mint is also supposed to deter rats and mice, but Randolph, who lives under my garden shed, seems to have become Mint-resistant, and thrives happily enough next to the Mint patch.

Midges and mosquitoes can be a serious deterrent to your gardening chores, if you have only the evenings in which to carry out such tasks. You can brew up a handful or two of Ground Elder and sponge yourself with the resulting liquid, but I rely on a dab of Oil of Citronella on the temples—very effective, and a little goes a long way. Mind you, it can repel humans as well, but that is a small price to pay.

Cats can be a serious problem in a small town garden, much as I love them, whereas, in larger gardens, there is plenty of room for them to co-exist with the plants and to keep away the mice and rats. A small collar with a bell will give the birds an Early Warning System and does not seem to bother the cat, which seems odd, when you think what tinnitus does to humans; if you put the cat's name, address and number on the collar, you are less likely to lose him. However, to protect your more precious young plants, sur-round them with sprigs of Holly, Gorse, Berberis or any other thorny subject, so that the cat will find it difficult to squat. These sprigs will have to be renewed from time to time, as they age and deteriorate like the rest of us, but they can then be added to the compost heap. They *do* work and they do not harm the cats, just keep them at paw's length, so to speak. A friend of mine was visited by the owner of a stately home, accompanied by a lion cub from their wildlife park. During lunch, the cub wandered around the garden, relieving himself from time to time, as is the way of such creatures. For six months my friend never had another cat come into her garden. They would leap onto the wall, freeze, spit out the cat's equivalent of 'Cripes!' and be off. If you do not have such grand friends, you could visit the local zoo and beg a few Big

Cat droppings from the keeper, which would probably have the same effect and could be added to the compost when past their best; this should astonish the worms. By the way, those nice red worms in the compost heap could be chopped and fed to your fish from time to time, as a bit of Roo's strengthening medicine.

Dogs may deter the cats, but they have their own disadvantages; bitches will scorch your lawn, dogs will choose something low and vulnerable on which to relieve themselves, unless carefully trained to go to a special place, a practice much recommended in training manuals, but ignored by all the dogs I know, who are rugged individualists. They will dig frantically under your fences to get at the cat next door, blunder through your flower borders in a fatuous attempt to catch butterflies and curl up to sleep on the seedlings, when they are not burying some obscene bone in the Rose bed. Taking them for long, exhausting walks will help to burn up their energy a bit, but yours will burn up faster. If you try tying them up on a long rope, out of reach of your more precious plants, they will howl heartrendingly until the RSPCA arrive. Life is full of such problems.

Birds present us with another difficult choice. A garden without them is an abomination, but if only they would show some restraint. I am quite prepared to share the garden produce with them, but not to hand it over entirely. My pleasure in the dawn chorus is diminished somewhat when I see the ravaged Primulas and Crocuses. I am reluctant to tie black cotton amongst things in case the birds become entangled, so I prefer to erect scarers of tinfoil and plastic strips over anything which needs protection; it does not do much good, but I feel I've tried. A cat scares them away for a while, and the dog barks at them, but that annoys me and my neighbours more than the birds, who treat him with the contempt he deserves or scold him roundly. In fact, I do as much as I can to *attract* birds to the garden, partly because they are such a delight, and also because they do help to keep a number of pests under control.

Hang lumps of fat from a piece of string tied to a cane and set this at a slant so that the fat hangs 30cm (1ft) above your Roses and 30cm (1ft) below the top of the cane. This prevents starlings reaching down from the cane or up from the Roses to munch all the fat before the tits, for whom it is intended, can get at it. You do this, not just out of the kindness of your heart, but because only a few tits can cling on to the fat ball at the same time. The rest in the queue will fill in the waiting time by finding greenfly eggs in the bark of the Rose bushes, which will save you a lot of spraying next summer. You can use the same system to discourage blackfly which overwinter in the Viburnums and Euonymus species. Tie the fat above these plants and do the birds and yourself a favour. Tie more fat in the branches of the Cherry trees, both fruiting and ornamental, for the same reason.

Hoverflies will produce larvae that are ferocious aphis-eaters, so the more hoverflies we can attract to our gardens, the better. According to Mr Lawrence Hills, whose books I cannot recommend too highly to impoverished gardeners, what hoverflies like best for breakfast is the pollen and nectar of the pretty little annual, *Convolvulus tricolor*, which does not share the distressing vices of its more familiar and rather common cousin, the Bindweed. Sow the seeds quite thinly in a sunny spot amongst the vegetables, or anywhere else where you have room for a few. Thin them out to about 15cm (6") apart and plant out the thinnings in another spot. The more hoverflies in your garden this year, the fewer aphides the next. Any that do survive can be sprayed with soapy water, or with a liquid you have made by simmering 454g (1lb) of the leaves of Rhubarb, Elder or Wormwood, in 1 litre (2 pints) of water for about half an hour and then diluting with one more litre (2 pints) of cold water. If you do buy the commercial sprays that claim to be safe, read the labels carefully and, to be on the side of the bees, spray after they have retired to bed, which is usually one hour before official sunset—but allow a little extra time, just in case.

If millipedes and wire worms are your problem, make a sneaky trap for them by piercing holes all round a tin, or make a cylinder of perforated metal. Fill this with potato peelings and sink it into the soil near any endangered species. It will be helpful to fit these traps with a handle of galvanised wire. Once a week haul up the traps and throw the mush to the chickens, if you have them, or flush down the loo if you have not. Do not add to the compost heap.

Slugs and snails can chomp through an alarming number of plants while you are asleep. You can foil them by surrounding anything that they particularly fancy with something rough and gritty, such as gravel, cinders, or crushed eggshells. Save up all your eggshells through the year so that you have a sufficient quantity to strew thickly when danger threatens. Lilies and Hostas come pretty high on the slugs' hit-list, so remember to give them a protective circle as soon as the young leaves appear. You can make slug-traps, too, by putting shallow dishes of beer and sugar, diluted half-and-half with water, at ground level in the garden overnight. The slugs will rush for this like city gents to a happy-hour, become equally sozzled, and eventually drown. Then they can be added to the compost heap and the trap refilled if necessary. Do not use plastic containers as the slugs can climb these; in fact the slugs in my garden make Sir Edmund Hillary look like a beginner. They get into the kitchen under the door *and* the draughtproofing, ascend the North Face of the Indesit and scale the dizzy heights of the double-oven, from whence they sneer at me when I come down for a mug of hot milk on sleepless nights; but pride goes before a fall and they are down the slim-line super-flush before they know it. If there are ghosts in this house, it will be those of the drowned slugs.

I hope I have impressed upon you the virtues of mulching your plants. It is unlikely that you will have enough compost to do this in large areas, so save that for plants that need it most. The same is true of leaf mould, unless you have a large garden on the edge of a forest. Lawn mowings are quite good, and if you do not like the look of them as they rot down, cover them with a sprinkling of earth. Old newspapers (or new ones, for that matter) make a good mulch and can be kept in place by stones, or pegged-down netting, and covered in the same way. Seaweed is another possibility if you are able to find some, and bracken is good, too. All of them should be applied when the soil is both warm and moist, not cold or dry.

Remember that wind can loosen plants and that even if they are not blown down they can be left loose and in danger. This can also happen after frost, so your tour of duty should include a check for this, firming down the soil and fixing stakes and ties. On the other hand, the ties may need to be let out on growing plants, as many a one has been damaged or killed by a forgotten tie which has bitten deeply into its stem. Even tree-ties made from nylon tights must be checked regularly, although they do have more 'give' than most.

If you do not have any sort of compost heap, do at least empty your tea-pots and tea-bags over the soil round any plants. Hydrangeas and Camellias seem particularly appreciative of this tonic, while, as I told you before, Roses will adore chopped-up banana skins as well as tea-leaves. Rinse out your milk bottles and pour the water over your plants as a diluted foliar feed and pick-me-up. Milk and yoghourt can be smeared over your pots and containers to encourage mosses and algae to grow there and 'age' them quickly.

If you have trees with ornamental bark, such as the Silver Birches and the Snake Bark Maples, you may find that they become covered with grime in towns and green gunge in the country, so give them a quick wash-and-brush-up with soapy water and a not too harsh scrubbing brush, to restore them to gleaming splendour. You should check all your trees and shrubs for dead wood and crossed branches that are chaffing. Cut these out as you notice them, or you will forget about them later. Neglected shrubs can often be revived by having one or two of their oldest branches cut right out. Shrub Roses, Lilacs and Privets are plants that will respond to this treatment, but be sure that you do not spoil the overall shape of the plant. Remember that any prunings (but not these old branches) are worth sticking in a bit of shady ground as cuttings, even if you do not attempt any serious propagation. This is also the time to see that your plants are not crowding each other out. Most youngish plants can be lifted and moved at almost any time of the year, if taken with a large enough root-ball and dragged on some kind of sheeting to a well-prepared new position. They will have to be regarded as convalescents for a while and perhaps given an overhead spray as well as regular waterings in dry weather. Evergreens can be sprayed with a special liquid to reduce the loss of moisture from their foliage. It is sold under different names, but is the stuff you put on the Christmas tree to prevent the needles dropping. I am glad to say that it works better on transplanted evergreens than it does on Christmas trees.

Overcrowding is obviously wasteful, and 'not 'ealthy, Ange,' as an old friend of mine used to say about almost everything in my life, from climbing plants on the house to socks in the mixed wash. It is difficult to get spacing right; one wants a casual, tumbling look, but not a confused mess, and no one gets it right all the time. Any bare patches can be filled by sowing with seed that you have gathered yourself (haven't you?), by house plants that need an airing, some vegetable seedling, or thinnings from elsewhere. *Gosh*, you are going to be busy; goodness knows how you are going to fit in the PTA and the Canadian Air-force exercises, let alone find the G spot . . .

When the weather is really too abominable for even the fanatical, do not imagine that you can just sit there by the fire and relax. There are gardening books to read, research to be done. The more books you can afford to buy, the more fun you will have and the more you will learn, but you can ask for the most expensive ones as a special present and search for others wherever secondhand books are to be found cheaply. Others you can borrow from the library, and at least this will do the poor authors a *bit* of good. Many of the cheap and cheerful gardening magazines are good value; look at them all and find one that suits you. They are rather less than the price of a 'single' in the average pub, and the pleasure they give will last considerably longer. Do not sneer at these periodicals. You might not necessarily feel tempted by the 'landscaped' gardens they illustrate, but they are full of practical up-to-date advice, economical hints and reliable information of all kinds. Your daily

and Sunday newspapers will almost certainly have a garden column and these, too, are very useful and virtually free, as you
would have bought the paper anyway; you can use them for
mulching, etc., afterwards as I have just pointed out, but cut out
the gardening bit first and file it away for future reference, if it is of
use or interest to you.

I would beg you to join the Royal Horticultural Society if you are
at all serious. Whatever the membership fee is by the time you read
this, it will be worth every penny. Not only do they have a monthly
magazine which is interesting, informative and easy to read, but
they have a library in which you can read or from which you can
borrow practically any book on gardening which is worth reading.
They have an advisory service, marvellous gardens at Wisley, and
regular shows at their two halls in Westminster. At the shows you
will often find plants for sale that you cannot obtain from the
average or even above-average garden centre, and those selling
them are usually only too happy to give you free advice and a
catalogue as well, for nothing or just a few pence. Members ask for
or offer seeds of rare plants in the Journal, as well as passing on the
information gained from years of experience through their letters.
Even if you are not yet a conservationist, you would find joining
the Soil Association worthwhile if you have a garden of more than a
few square yards. They, too, have a magazine, and several book-
lets which give you the latest information and tips on organic
gardening, many of which are of a very economical nature. In
addition to all this, lots of bulb and seed catalogues are free, if you
bother to fill in the little coupons in the gardening press. Not only
are they pleasant reading but often full of useful information, and
you can use the photographs to help you plan out your garden in
the way that I described in Chapter 2.

When I began this book, I was not sure whether I would be able
to find enough things to say about economy in the garden, but now
I am finding it quite difficult to stop, as you may have noticed. I do
hope that you have found at least some of it helpful . . . Oh, and
another thing . . .

USEFUL ADDRESSES

The Royal Horticultural Society,
Vincent Square,
Westminster,
London SW1 2PE.

For practically everything, so
that you can forgive them the
terrible flower arrangement
classes at their shows.

The Soil Association,
86–88 Colston Street,
Bristol BS1 5BB.

For organic gardening
information and techniques.

The Henry Doubleday Research
  Association,
National Centre for Organic
Gardening,
Wolston,
Coventry,
West Midlands.

Ditto.

Turning Worms,
Unit 42,
Glan-yr-Afon Industrial Estate,
Llanbadarn,
Aberystwyth,
Dyfed,
Wales.

For organic seed and potting
composts manufactured by
worms. You can also order
starter kits of worm eggs and
suitable material with
instructions on establishing
your own back garden fertiliser
factory.

The National Trust,
42 Queen Anne's Gate,
London SW1.

To see how it is done on the
grand scale. Compulsive for
nosey-parkers.

BOOK LIST

GENERAL REFERENCE
The Dictionary of Garden Plants in Colour by Roy Hay and Patrick M. Synge. Ebury Press and Michael Joseph, 1969.
The Dictionary of Roses in Colour by S. Miller Gault and Patrick M. Synge. Mermaid Books, 1985.
Reader's Digest Encyclopaedia of Garden Plants and Flowers, second edition. Reader's Digest Association, 1978.
The Gardening Year. Reader's Digest Association, 1976.
The RHS Encyclopaedia of Practical Gardening. Mitchell Beazley, 1981.
The Wisley Handbooks. The Royal Horticultural Society in association with Cassell. (These small, inexpensive books cover a wide range of subjects and are all worth having, according to your interests.)
The New Small Garden by C. E. Lucas-Phillips. Pan Books, 1979.
Hillier's Manual of Trees and Shrubs, fourth edition. David and Charles, 1977.

FOR PLANNING, CONSTRUCTION AND GENERAL INFORMATION
Anything and everything by John Brookes, especially *The Garden Book* (Dorling Kindersley, 1984) and *Room Outside* (Thames and Hudson, 1969).
Garden Projects. Windward Press, 1985.

FOR INSPIRATION BACKED BY SOUND KNOWLEDGE
Anything by Christopher Lloyd, especially *The Well-Tempered Garden* (revised edition, Viking, 1985).
Any of Beverley Nichols' gardening books (yes, really).

Anything by Margery Fish, Beth Chatto and Graham Stuart Thomas, especially his Rose books.

FOR ORGANIC GARDENING, ETC.

Anything by Lawrence D. Hills, especially *Organic Gardening* (Penguin Books, 1977) and *Down to Earth Gardening* (Faber Paperbacks, 1975).

Old Wives' Lore for Gardeners by Maureen and Bridget Boland. Bodley Head, 1976.

Composting by Dick Kitto. Thorsons, 1984.

Nature on Your Side by Greet Buchner and Fieke Hoogvelt. Pan Books, 1978.

Companion Plants by Helen Philbrick and Richard B. Gregg. Watkins.

SPECIALIST

Water Gardening by Frances Perry. Country Life, 1938.

The Garden Pool by Frances Perry. Collingridge, 1951.

The Water Garden by H. L. V. Fletcher. John Lehmann, 1951.

The Water Garden by Gordon T. Ledbetter. Alphabooks, 1984.

The Book of Patios and Ponds by Gordon T. Ledbetter. Alphabooks, 1984.

Wild Flowers in the Garden by W. E. Th. Ingwersen. Geoffrey Bles, 1951.

The Concise British Flora in Colour by W. Keble Martin. Sphere Books, 1979.

Gardening in Window Boxes and other Containers by H. L. V. Fletcher. Pelham Books, 1969.

The Contained Garden by K. A. Becket, David Carr and David Stevens. Sphere Books, 1983.

Town and City Gardening by Michael Miller (formerly called *Not Just Small but Tiny*). Chancellor Press, 1985.

Be Your Own . . . Expert books by Dr D. G. Hessayon. pbi publications. (Incredibly cheap, and you do not *have* to use all the pbi products he mentions.)

Gardening on Chalk and Lime by Ronald Dyson. Dent, 1977.
A Chalk Garden by F. C. Stern. Nelson, 1960.
Anything by Joy Larkcom on vegetable gardening, etc.

INDEX